Gifts of the Great Spirit

Volume IV

...Legends...

Managing Editor: Barbara Callahan Quin
Contributing Editor: Wanda Sue Parrott

Published by

Great Spirit Publishing

Springfield, Missouri
greatspiritpublishing@yahoo.com

independent publishing technologies

ISBN-13: 978-1490916200
ISBN-10: 1490916202

Printed in USA

DEDICATION

To The Great Spirit, first and foremost,
the Creator of All Life,
with gratitude for the beauty and
inspiration shared on these pages.

To our 2013 White Buffalo Native American
Poet Laureate contributors.

To our Dream Catcher Literary
Challenge contributors.

To our Readers and Supporters
from around the world.

Thank You.

Aho!

ACKNOWLEDGMENTS

The editors wish to acknowledge and thank everyone who
participated in our White Buffalo Native American
Poet Laureate poetry contest and "Legends" literary challenge.
We also wish to acknowledge Wanda Sue Parrott and her
Amy Kitchener's Angels Without Wings Foundation
(www.amykitchenerfdn.org) –
it is because of her countless hours of organization
and management of the contest that we are able to
provide this Volume IV edition.

This edition features the poetry of the
2013 White Buffalo Native American
Poet Laureate Gail Denham,
and two White Buffalo Calf Award winners,
Carol Leavitt Altieri and Lee Pelham Cotton, and winners of
nine online awards, plus the "Legends" literary challenge
contributors also included in this book.

We hope you enjoy reading these poems and tributes
honoring the Great Spirit which resides within us all.

2013 White Buffalo Native American Poet Laureate Poetry Contest Winners

2013 White Buffalo Native American Poet Laureate:
"We Run, the Deer and I" by Gail Denham

2013 White Buffalo Native American Calf Awards:
"Molly Ockett, Indian Doctress" by Carol Leavitt Altieri
"White Man's Foot, White Man's Flies" by Lee Pelham Cotton

**2013 White Buffalo Native American Peace Pipe
Honorable Mention Awards:**
"Who Will Speak" by Ella Cather-Davis
"Patience" by Gail Denham

2013 White Buffalo Native American Chief's Choice Awards:
"Explorers" by Dr. Charles A. Stone
"A Shawnee's Lifestyle" by Helen Webb

2013 White Buffalo Native American Silver Sage Online Awards:
"Eagle Song" by Elaine P. Morgan
"Someone is Listening" by Ella Cather-Davis
"Our Native American Ancestors Are With Us Always"
   by Barbara Youngblood Carr
"Today... At The Pow Wow" by Juan Manuel Perez
"Still the Whippoorwill Calls" by Yvonne Nunn

2013
White Buffalo
Native American
Poet Laureate
Poetry Contest
Winners

2013 White Buffalo Native American Poet Laureate

Gail Denham

For more than thirty-five years, **Gail Denham's** short stories, essays, poetry, news articles, and photography have appeared in a wide variety of national and international publications. Gail's passion lies in writing of the "real" – telling stories, and sharing humor. She belongs to a number of state poetry associations and enjoys entering contests, taking the challenge to meet themes and interpret ideas. Gail revels in exploring the world where she lives, Central Oregon, a natural paradise of spoken and felt history, ancient juniper, and stories told by wind-blown pines. She and her husband have four sons and fourteen grandchildren. Gail leads writing and photography workshops at Pacific Northwest writers' conferences.

Gail joins prior White Buffalo poets laureate Barbara Youngblood Carr (2009), Dr. Carl B. Reed (2010), Dr. Charles A. Stone (2011), and Neal "Badger Bob White" Whitman (2012) as Honorary Chiefs of the White Buffalo Tribe.

WE RUN, THE DEER AND I

...after "Pocahontas" by Annie Leibovitz

Gail Denham

Hair, black as caves; eyes, full of forest. Why this loose
captivity—leading pale, whiskered men who brag of free
land. I wonder. What do they covet? All streams, trees,
fish, deer meat offerings, mountains are free to every man.
The people, my people, roam and give thanks for it all.

These hated men, wearing more daily clothes than the old
women of the tribe shivering under their blankets in freezing
winter winds. Trying to hack through thick river woods,
these over-dressed men with their buttons and clasps
become stuck on branches, trip over bushes.

And the food. If my grandmother hadn't given that man,
called Clark, lessons on preparing quick root vegetable stew,
using forest tubers, the company would starve. The small
packet of herbs grandmother sent with me dwindles daily.
Secretly I sprinkle some on my bowl each night,
as I thank the forest and eat.

Right now I must run, race with my deer friends,
feel fresh air on my face, away from the smell of boatfuls
of men, full of talk, so filled with importance and seeming
to know the world, my world. The deer and I know. We run
and laugh. Other creatures cheer us from the trees.

They know the answers.

MOLLY OCKETT, INDIAN DOCTRESS
Carol Leavitt Altieri

I was born on a spit of land below Saco Falls in Maine. Indian Island some called it, and I never knew the year, though I was around fifteen at the time of Rogers' raid on St. Francis Mission in Quebec in 1759.

My father and grandfather were chiefs who survived the colonial wars, sometimes on the French side but more often on the English. In the Androscoggin Valley, I lived with a small party of Indians

who joined mixed colonists - wintering with them in the cave we dug by the river. At times, I was called to help cure settlers' dysentery. For that, I used a blend of inner bark of spruce.

I nursed many sick people back to health and acted as a midwife for birth of a white child. For my cures, I used roots, herbs, barks, and potions. Near my cave, I found Solomon's Seal and pounded its roots to treat wounds.

I shared some concoctions, but others I would not reveal. Henry Tufts called me the great Indian doctress. Others saw me cloaked with magic powers. Hannibal Hamlin, too, was one of my healed ones who grew up to be a vice-president.

Some thought of me as a witch even though I had close friendships with many settlers and cured many of their illnesses. I had Catholic ties and attended Protestant services, not being bound by religious conventions.

If they tried to turn me away, I would find a stool and sit in front of the altar. Once, I buried a cache of possessions on Hemlock Island and a thief stole them. I soon recognized my hatchet in the culprit's home and placed a curse on him.

If settlers tried to take our land, I scared them with foretelling dark July days so hot that water would boil in their wells, glass melt in the windows, and farm animals would die from drought.

My reputation grew as I tried to bring the settlers and Indians together, teaching them basketry, moccasin-making, pottery, and weaving. I fell ill in the spring of 1815 and my Indian groups stayed with me until they had to leave, hunt, and fish.

During my last months, I knew that I would die soon. I insisted on dying in a camp of fragrant cedar and was pleased that Captain Bragg built one for me. I'd learned that I didn't have the strength to carry on and I knew I always walked a straight path and was the last of the Pequawkets. Over in the farmland, the cornfield's blazing spread like a conflagration.

My religion is from the Great Spirit. I followed the Biblical verse from Matthew: Straight is the gate, and narrow is the way that leadeth to life eternal; and few there are that find it.

Carol Leavitt Altieri is a retired environmental science and language arts teacher from Madison, Connecticut. She is 2011 Senior Poet Laureate for Connecticut, and author of four books of poetry and recipient of the State of Connecticut's "Green Circle Award" for environmental stewardship. She has two children. Carol enjoys her grandchildren, hiking, biking, birding, traveling, and reading.

WHITE MAN'S FOOT, WHITE MAN'S FLIES
Lee Pelham Cotton

white man's foot and white man's flies
plantain green, bee gold in flight
far to the west our village lies

the bee, a-buzz with laden thighs
a golden, honey-making wight
white man's foot and white man's flies

plantain's broad leaves that soothe sore eyes
appear like footprints formed in night
and to the west our village lies

deer, at queer humming, starts and shies
but soon crops plantain with delight
white man's foot and white man's flies

bear, drawn by sweetness, utters cries
its greedy raiding turned to flight
not far from where our village lies

they're here to stay, these feet and flies
like iron axe and glass beads bright
white man's foot and white man's flies
surrounded thus our village lies

n.b. Thomas Jefferson, in Notes on the State of Virginia, observed that Virginia Indians knew that when the white man's flies (i.e. bees) arrived at a hitherto remote village, the colonists were not far away. White man's foot is a name given by native peoples to the prolific, broad-leafed greater plantain (Plantago major), also introduced by the English.

Lee Pelham Cotton (shown here with her pug Figaro) lives with her husband and four rescue dogs in an old farmhouse a few miles from the Chesapeake Bay. An interpretive park ranger at Historic Jamestowne, Lee shares the story of Pocahontas and her people with visitors of all ages from all over the world. Her poems have appeared in  numerous publications and she currently writes "Creature Comforts," a column for *Crone*, a magazine for uppity older women.

WHO WILL SPEAK
Ella Cather-Davis

Hear me now.

Today, over three million Native American exist;
564 tribes who believe in a manifest destiny.
They are the Earth people whose quest is to
search within, discover daily a changing spirit, and
to understand their connection to the unseen.

Wakan Tanka tells them that peace comes
when the soul realizes its oneness
with both the Universe and all of life,
both the two-legged and four-legged.

Who will speak?

Not the frenzied entrepreneur selling his ideas,
nor the ceaseless News chatterer, with *his* truth.
No, not these.

Listen to the coyote, the eagle, gray owl,
moon woman, the buffalo, the black bear,
frog and cricket, the storm, sacred water,
the stars, the wind, the quiet.

Store up the truth given by the Great Spirit,
to the ant, the bee, the cactus, the stone, the butterfly,
all these who open our eyes to the circle of light
where four winds meet.
These. These shall speak – with no words.

Listen

PATIENCE
Gail Denham

Rivers take their time. A spring
trickles from under a mountain lip.
Soon gravity brings other streams.

The river grows larger, plows through
a hill. It is patient. Years pass. Crevices
appear. Storms dig wider slits.

Rocks crumble. Steady flow carves
canyons. River believes in the ocean.
It feels its power grow.

Each droplet, every ripple sings joy.
The eddies and small wavelets
are satisfied. Clouds add more moisture.

Over the canyon, past the streamlets,
rains let loose near the first hill's seepage.
Down river, waves roar with pride.

EXPLORERS
Dr. Charles A. Stone

Quiet as a field of wildflowers,
we search the forest of the sea island
for familiar trees, for signal stones from prior visits.

Leather moccasins stuff against fossil shells
which line dry creek beds or luxuriate in opaque pools
as we sidestep footprints of terrible lizards
who ruled here when rocks were still mud.

Where Mother's stony spine leans onto a sandy beach,
littered with bodies of sea grasses and bones of trees
which stood too close to the surging surf,
we pause in our descent of the slippery slope
to admire the green upon green of leaves
and vines and evergreens, to wonder at Mother's purpose
in studding the island's verdant fortress walls with
star-bright asters, purple wood violets, and wine-red phlox,
to marvel at the horizon where the topaz sky melts
into deep aquamarine sea.

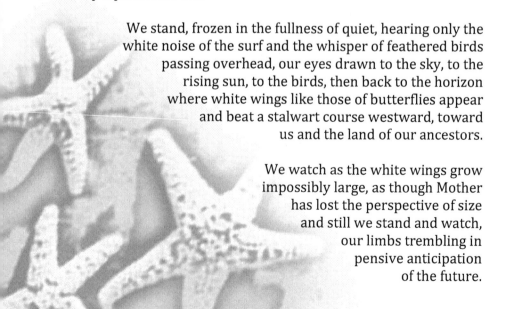

We stand, frozen in the fullness of quiet, hearing only the
white noise of the surf and the whisper of feathered birds
passing overhead, our eyes drawn to the sky, to the
rising sun, to the birds, then back to the horizon
where white wings like those of butterflies appear
and beat a stalwart course westward, toward
us and the land of our ancestors.

We watch as the white wings grow
impossibly large, as though Mother
has lost the perspective of size
and still we stand and watch,
our limbs trembling in
pensive anticipation
of the future.

A SHAWNEE'S LIFESTYLE
Helen Webb

If you had been born a Shawnee son
You would have been named within ten days;
If a daughter, within twelve.
Social classification was the chief consideration
For selection of the name.
No surnames were used.
Mothers carried babies on backboards
With their heads strapped to the boards.
This formed a flat surface to which a plate
Mounted with feathers or other ornamentation
Could be affixed with a headband.

Shawnee children grew up as free
As the animals that roamed their forests.
Boys engaged in running, jumping,
Swimming, and archery practice.
They never played with girls,
And from a very early age
Developed a sense of superiority
Even over their own sisters.
The girls, not minding, played house, developed skills
In molding clay vessels and in basket weaving.

The Shawnee men were hunters and warriors.
The women did all the domestic work.
They also cared for the tribe's ailments,
Were skilled in mixing herbs and setting bones.

Shawnees believed in a supreme being, Moneto,
Who blessed all earning his favor
And cursed those meriting disfavor.
Their "Golden Rule," preserved by
Joseph Wildcat Alford, is much like ours:
"Do not kill or injure your neighbor,

For it is not him that you injure, you injure yourself.
But do good to him, therefore add to his days
Of happiness as you add to your own.
Do not wrong or hate your neighbor,
For it is not him that you wrong, you wrong yourself.
But love him, for Moneto loves him also as he loves you."

One of their great chiefs, Tecumseh,
Envisioned creation of one Indian nation.
He worked hard to unite the tribes
Against the advancing whites,
But his dream was doomed when he met defeat
In the battle of Tippecanoe.

OUR NATIVE AMERICAN ANCESTORS
ARE WITH US ALWAYS
Barbara Youngblood Carr

Memories blow on the wind
through canyons and valleys
and the lands of our Fathers,
Grandfathers and others
of our Native American ancestors.

> Because the Great Spirit
> shaped them from rich, red clay,
> when they touch the earth
> it sings with the beauty
> of all natural treasures.

Like smoke from peace pipes,
they whisper into sunsets.
Their chants sing through trees,
sink into deep river's
harmonious currents,
travel to everywhere.

Their spirits color rainbows,
fall trees and butterflies,
travel with forest–totem
creatures, create ghostly rhythms
of beating wings and drums
that give our lives cadence.

Their ghosts
straddle the moon and stars,
ride them into the night sky.
Their glitter lights our trails
on earth so we can walk
forward into our own
destinies.

EAGLE SONG
Elaine P. Morgan

The forest in the early morning. Trees barren
of leaves, anorexic against the canvas of a
slate gray sky. A mockingbird sips rain
drops from a dried oak leaf. Lone hawk
tilts its head upwards, wings outstretched,
worshipping the retreating rays of the tepid
winter sun. Canada Geese herald their
journey to the icy water of the lake. Two
swoop and skim the forest floor, levitating
in poetic choreography.

He walks in the shadows of sunlight.
Phantoms dance in darkness, resurrected
in the lukewarm splintered sun. He awakes
and dreams of dead crows shouting revelry.
Great Spirit calls his name, saying, Do not
weep. You are not alone. Shake the rattle.
They may return. Old Shaman giggles,
knowing life is paradoxical. He chases all
the ghosts away with one sweep of his
whispering eagle wing.

A rainbow filters through a crystal prism,
coloring his outer world. He's a child again,
lying in a field of rattling corn stalks, eyes
closed, watching colored lights. The moon
waxes between his brows. He sings in his
sleep and flies in his dreams. A one-eyed
wounded healer waiting to take flight
as a million winking stars light the hole
in the sky and the floor of the earth.

He hears the scream of an eagle and
realizes he is not alone. A Spirit flies
the banner of itself, chanting a Shaman song.
He does not hear himself sing. He does not
hear himself sing. He whispers as softly as
the wink of the eyelid of an owl. As gently
as the flutter of the wing of a butterfly. He
whispers like the sweep of the wing of an
eagle as it takes flight.

SOMEONE IS LISTENING
Ella Cather-Davis

The moon glows in the inky sky directly above
and the fire ring, glowing embers, leaps
in an undulating orange, yellow, and blue dance.
Frog and cricket are singing a duet.

Why would an Asteroid impact destroy Earth?
Would it be the change of axis, is it inevitable?
We take turns wondering what will happen.
How does this work scientifically?

Will we all suddenly be upside down?
Will we fall off the face of earth?
Will we be whirled into the surface
of the nuclear sun and disintegrate?

Frog and cricket raise their voices insistently,
Fire dances wildly and we at last concede:
Some things are too big to understand –
too vast to wrap our human brain around.

I look up to love the moon and there it is,
wreathed with a perfect circle of swirling
clouds round its façade, a veritable vortex.
Someone is listening.

STILL THE WHIPPOORWILL CALLS
Yvonne Nunn

At dark the call of whippoorwills
alerts a sprawling domicile
two miles between two Deep Creek hills.

Like Peyote scouts of long ago
announced approach of wandering Crow.

The sound is like a lullaby,
enchants nocturnal passerby
yet calls in code to pacify.

A Daniel Boone could do no less
than mock the bird in moves of chess.

As echo of redundant past
brings then two now in roles recast
in movies where the blood runs fast.

Aghast at white man's sole controls,
the war whoops scream from burial knolls.

Still whippoorwills make trills in sounds
where cattle roam in fenced in bounds
across the sunken native mounds.

TODAY... AT THE POW WOW
Juan Manuel Perez

As the gourd dancer dances
To bless all things to pure
And the sun sunshines
On all that they endure

As the big-drum drums
Where all the nations gather
As the One-Son's father
Tries to stop his children's tatter

As they sweat, sweet sweats
Dancing their sins away
As the people take a breath
Watching the sun pass the day

As the sun passes the day
As the son passes today

2013

Literary Challenge

"Legends"

2013 White Buffalo Native American Literary Challenge Contributions

"Shadows" by Elayne Azevedo

"Grandfather's Secret" by Wanda Sue Parrott

"Black Elk Speaks" by Jonathan Shoemaker

"The Real World" by Black Elk

"Maidens, Pale-face Bison and the Wind" by Carol Dee Meeks

"Legends Live On" by Vincent J. Tomeo

"Alaska by Boat, by Gawd" by Neal "Badger Bob White" Whitman

"If Nature Held a Garage Sale" by The Late Robert D. Hoeft

"Story of the Peace Pipe"

"Blessing for a Sick World"

"No Tears, Just Quiet Reflection" by Linda Amos

"Naming Water" by Carol Willette Bachofner

"The Mother of All of the People"

"Native American Dreamer" by Vera Jane Goodin Schultz

"Warrior's Song" by Renee Meador

"Redeem the Truth" by Harold E. Grice

"Warriors of the Rainbow"

"Pow Wow Time" by Judy Olson Mosca

"Dissipating Vision" by Cindy Bechtold

"Shadow, My Dream Guide" by Yvonne Londres

"White Man Teacher" by Houstine Cooper

"The Beginning of Time"

"Flight of the Fin and Feather" by Barbara Callahan Quin

"Ahiga's Quest" by Madeline McEwen

"The Sacred Earth"

"In the Gila Monster Den" by William Childress

"My Mouse" by Doreen Lindahl

"Reflections on a Silhouette: Great Spirits Live On" by Vincent J. Tomeo

"Boss of the Wilderness" by Carol Dee Meeks

"The Forgotten Ear of Corn"

"Light Warrior" by Cindy M. Hutchings

"How the Fawn Got Its Spots"

"Forgive Everyone Everything" by Judy Olson Mosca

"The Legend of Glisten Trail" by Yvonne Londres

"Trail of Time" by Neal "Badger Bob White" Whitman

LEGENDS – Fact or Fiction?

People everywhere have been enchanted with Native American legends since the first white man and red man made contact, whether in peacetime or at war. Each Native American tribe has its own history, its own version of how creation came about and how to live in harmony with the earth. Who can say whether these stories are fact or fiction? Our purpose here is not to prove a legend one way or the other, but to share a viewpoint from our writers in the Native American voice as inspired by the Great Spirit.

We do not place emphasis on any one traditional tribe over another, nor any viewpoint over another. We believe in the ultimate Tribe of Oneness, the Tribe of All Humanity, which exists by the grace of the Great Spirit (Creator/God), and in a territory where there are no boundaries and no borders between peoples, where all life is sacred. There is an element of universal truth in all Native American legends and we hope you are inspired by reading the poetry and prose shared here in this very special **Legends** edition of *Gifts of the Great Spirit*. We will leave personal interpretation to the reader. *Aho!*

White Buffalo Calf Woman*

White Buffalo Calf Woman

Long ago, there was a time of famine. The chief of the Lakota sent two scouts out to hunt for food. As the young men travelled, they saw a figure in the distance. As they approached they saw that it was a beautiful young woman in white clothing. One of the men was filled with desire for the woman. He approached her, telling his companion he would attempt to embrace the woman, and if he found her pleasing, he would claim her as a wife. His companion warned him that she appeared to be a sacred woman, and to do anything sacrilegious would be folly. The man ignored the other's advice.

The companion watched as the other approached and embraced the woman, during which time a white cloud enveloped the pair. After a while, the cloud disappeared and only the mysterious woman and a pile of bones remained. The remaining man was frightened, and began to draw his bow, but the woman beckoned him forward, telling him that no harm would come to him. As the woman spoke Lakota, the young man decided she was one of his people, and came forward. When he arrived, she pointed to a spot on the ground where the other scout's bare bones lay. She explained that the Crazy Buffalo had compelled the man to desire her, and she had annihilated him.

The man became even more frightened and again menaced her with his bow. At this time, the woman explained that she was *wakan* (holy) and his weapons could not harm her. She further explained that if he did as she instructed, no harm would befall him and that his tribe would become more prosperous. The scout promised to do what she instructed, and was told to return to his encampment, call the Council and prepare a feast for her arrival.

The woman's name was *PtesanWi*, which translates to *White Buffalo Calf Woman*. She taught the Lakota seven sacred rituals and gave them the *chanupa*, or sacred pipe, which is the holiest of all worship symbols. After teaching the people and giving them her gifts, *PtesanWi* left them, promising to return again. ❖

SHADOWS
Elayne Marie Azevedo

Night wakes as shadows rise and fall
Luminous clouds dance upon the sky
And two clay pillars deeply rooted in the Earth
Step beat by beat.
Aroused in Life's rhythmic pulse
Strong kindled arms cradle the day
With open palms shifting light as curtains fall
An offering is made from Earth to Sky
A pause in radiant light transforms
Gray hues dull pain and suffering
Shadows glows with gratitude
And a humble prayer puts the day to sleep
❖

GRANDFATHER'S SECRET

Wanda Sue Parrott

The Iowa Territory around 1830
as inspired by Amy Kitchener (1820-1889)

When the old Sioux died, something amazing happened. Instead of tottering on shaking legs, he leaped like a running hare from his body, then shape-shifted to a dust devil that whirled to face the corpse. "That's not me," he thought in Lakota.

He recognized the grizzled man children of the tribe called Tunkashila *(toon-ka-sila)*, meaning "everyone's grandfather," and his white settler friend Cyrus called "Indian Moses" because he was speculative about God.

The two men were the eldest of their respective families in the Iowa Territory. They hunted rabbits, smoked tobacco, and tried to learn one another's language by arguing religion. The white man told Mose about Heaven. He taught Cyrus about the Happy Hunting Ground. Neither knew whether there really was existence after death. All he knew was he was very much alive now and the old man before him was dead.

He mused, "That old Indian looks like the image I saw in the looking glass Cyrus swapped for the runt pup I gave him. But he was in so much pain, he groaned each time his wife dragged him outside on his blanket to die. I am fine. I feel like I can fly." He sprang skyward, landing in a young hunter's crouch, without wincing from a single shin splint.

He knew Red Feather had propped her ailing spouse against dry stalks of sun-dried yellow corn. The kernels would be harvested for next season's planting if the crows didn't get them first, so the corn shocks served both as walls against which to set up the feeble, infirm and dying so they would act as scarecrows; and as spiritual launch areas from which the dead could easily ascend into the sky before their remains were buried to feed the earth a day after death, or devoured by scavengers under the moon.

Gazing at the black eyes now staring like white man's buckshot into the sun, he said, "If you are dead, go on. Rise into the sky!"

He extended his arm and shoved the warm corpse's shoulder. His whole hand went through the chest of the deceased. He pulled it back out and shook transparent wispy fingers. They glowed with the same silvery sheen as a thread gleaming like a spider's web that was connecting the corpse's breast with his own heart as if it were a papoose's umbilical cord connected to its mother after birth.

He moved sideways and the filament stretched.

He backed away. The string expanded.

He moved near the corpse. The strand shrank.

Just then a dozen moccasin-makers, who had been washing deerskin at the river, ambled toward the row of cornstalks on which to stretch their strips to dry.

"Hello, Red Feather," he said to the old man's wife. She looked toward her dead husband's eyes, gasped, and then dropped her pelts in the dust. She began hiccoughing and moaning. Her wails shrilled to a keening shriek that attracted attention of the other women and a few roaming dogs. A spotted bitch with milk-sodden teats and only three legs howled a mournful cry. Other dogs and humans joined in. The shrill sounds hurt his mind.

"Red Feather, my beloved, calm down!" He tried to joke as the frenzy grew and dust arose. "You mighten wake the dead!"

A look of horror crossed her face, as if she had heard a ghost. She gazed through him as she tenderly closed the glassing eyes of the man who could no longer see. Her hand sliced through the diaphanous silver thread connecting the men. It snapped. The corpse stiffened like instant setting stone. The Sioux spirit jerked free, trembling.

A blinding flash of white light filled his consciousness. Despite efforts to stay grounded, he was catapulted into the sky. The scene beneath him grew smaller and dimmer as he drifted toward his white friend's Sun of God known as Christ and his own People's Great Spirit known as White Buffalo.

Suddenly he understood the esoteric secret neither he nor Cyrus could resolve, and he exclaimed in a jittery joyful jumble of Lakota and English, "Well, I'll be danged. I've shape-shifted. I can soar. I can see. I AM Eagle!" ❖

"Regard Heaven as your Father, Earth as your Mother,
and all things as your Brothers and Sisters."
~ *Native American Proverb*

BLACK ELK SPEAKS
Jonathan Shoemaker

The Creator dwells in the core of the earth;
In the core of each one of us He dwells.
In each creature's heart dwells the Spirit of God,
The spring from which peaceful compassion wells.

Compassion and peace from the heart of each;
Peace and compassion toward others.
Peace in one's heart, from which we impart
True compassion toward each of our brothers.

And if we want peace among all mankind,
Among all the nations of the earth, we must start
Showing peace and compassion, from one to the other.
But first we must each feel true peace in our hearts.

This message from Black Elk comes down through the years.
Let us share in his wisdom, and not in his tears.

THE REAL WORLD
~ Black Elk, Lakota, 1863-1950

"Men die but live again
in the real world of Wakan-Tanka,
where there is nothing but
the spirits of all things;
and this true life
we may know here on earth
if we purify our bodies and minds
thus coming closer to Wakan-Tanka
who is all-purity."

❖

Image source: Department of Defense via Public Domain Clip Art
(www. publicdomainclip-art.blogspot.com)

MAIDENS, PALE-FACE BISON AND THE WIND

Carol Dee Meeks

Whenever windstorms blow 'cross canyon rims,
a secret puffs above a maiden's hair;
her fashioned buckskin boots have turquoise brims
and matching beaded feathers carve the air.

Whenever windstorms blow throughout the night,
the maiden takes a walk for knowledge gain;
the wind explains her clan may face a fight
unless a bison spirit bolts to reign.

Whenever windstorms blow near mountain's edge,
again, the maiden kneels on sacred ground
where she salutes the paler wisent's* pledge,
who tells the tribe their fate from breeze and sound.

Whenever windstorms blow through cacti spikes,
the thickets sway like tunes Contankas** play
along the trail the natives use for hikes;
good fortune dwells until the *pale-ones* stray.

*Wisent – another word for buffalo
**Contanka – an Indian flute

LEGENDS LIVE ON
Vincent J. Tomeo

Black shadow you have cast a silhouette
that dominates the horizon like blue thunder
Out of ruffled blue –white clouds you stepped forward
in your moccasins, your footprints kicking up dust on the Great Plains
standing up to the ghost of yesterday's tomorrow

Your legends posted on the front page of magazines
Noble brave your footprints obscured
yet the echo of your drums still throbs
long after the beating has stopped
Hear the galloping horses
See the rising Sun

"Wisdom comes only when you stop looking for it and start
living the life the Creator intended for you."
~ Native American Proverb ~ Hopi

ALASKA BY BOAT, BY GAWD
Neal "Badger Bob White" Whitman

layered green slopes
topped with wreath of mist
the Inside Passage
Queen Charlotte's Sound
the passing current
silent
Alaska's sunset
a long bridge from dusk
to dark

IF NATURE HELD A GARAGE SALE
The Late Robert D. Hoeft

You could buy small oceans
Only slightly used by whales,
Deserts with lots of good sand
Left in them, old mountains
Still high enough to provide
A splendid view, rain clouds
With ample drops remaining
To give a few good showers.

But it's the seasons I would want,
Summers shabby in old boxes
That when unwrapped would ooze
Multiple days of sunshine;
Apparently tepid winters
Carelessly packed in trunks
When unpacked would spew snowflakes
In tennis-court size blizzards;
Autumns, drab with dust, when taken home
Would radiate enough colors
To make your own rainbow,
And a spring, high on a cobweb shelf,
With only a little polishing,
Would gleam with enough hope
To light me to the end of my days.

❖

STORY OF THE PEACE PIPE

Two young men were out strolling one night talking of love affairs. They passed around a hill and came to a little ravine or coulee. Suddenly they saw coming up from the ravine a beautiful woman. She was painted and her dress was of the very finest material.

"What a beautiful girl!" said one of the young men. "Already I love her. I will steal her and make her my wife."

"No," said the other. "Don't harm her. She may be holy."

The young woman approached and held out a pipe which she first offered to the sky, then to the earth and then advanced, holding it out in her extended hands.

"I know what you young men have been saying; one of you is good; the other is wicked," she said.

She laid down the pipe on the ground and at once became a buffalo cow. The cow pawed the ground, stuck her tail straight out behind her and then lifted the pipe from the ground again in her hoofs; immediately she became a young woman again.

"I am come to give you this gift," she said. "It is the peace pipe. Hereafter all treaties and ceremonies shall be performed after smoking it. It shall bring peaceful thoughts into your minds. You shall offer it to the Great Mystery and to mother earth."

The two young men ran to the village and told what they had seen and heard. The entire village came out where the young woman was.

She repeated to them what she had already told the young men and added:

"When you set free the ghost (the spirit of deceased persons) you must have a white buffalo cow skin."

She gave the pipe to the medicine men of the village, turned again to a buffalo cow and fled away to the land of buffaloes.

From Native American Encyclopedia, used via Creative Commons Attribution/Share-Alike License 3.0 (Source: legendsofamerica)

CRAZY HORSE'S BLESSING FOR A SICK WORLD

"The Red Nation shall rise again and it shall be a blessing for a sick world; a world filled with broken promises, selfishness and separations; a world longing for light again.

"I see a time of Seven Generations when all the colors of mankind will gather under the Sacred Tree of Life and the whole Earth will become one circle again.

"In that day, there will be those among the Lakota who will carry knowledge and understanding of unity among all living things and the young white ones will come to those of my people and ask for this wisdom.

"I salute the light within your eyes where the whole Universe dwells. For when you are at that center within you and I am that place within me, we shall be one."

~ Crazy Horse, Oglala Lakota Sioux (circa 1840-1877)

Crazy Horse is quoted as saying this (above) while he sat smoking the Sacred Pipe with Sitting Bull for the last time. Crazy Horse was killed four days later by US Army soldiers in a hand-to-hand scuffle as they attempted to imprison him. There are no known photographs of Crazy Horse, he would not permit anyone to take his picture, presumably because Crazy Horse believed a photograph stole or unnaturally held the soul of the person(s) pictured.

(*Source: http://www.californiaindianeducation.org/famous_indian_chiefs/*)

BLACK ELK TELLS HOW CRAZY HORSE GOT HIS NAME

A contemporary tribesman and cousin of Crazy Horse, in his classic text, Black Elk Speaks: being the life story of a holy man of the Oglala Sioux was said to provide an account of Crazy Horse's vision from which he derived his name.

"When I was a man, my father told me something about that vision. Of course he did not know all of it; but he said that Crazy Horse dreamed and went into the world where there is nothing but the spirits of all things. That is the real world that is behind this one, and everything we see here is something like a shadow from that world. He was on his horse in that world, and the horse and himself on it and the trees and the grass and the stones and everything were made of spirit, and nothing was hard, and everything seemed to float. His horse was standing still there, and yet it danced around like a horse made only of shadow, and that is how he got his name, which does not mean that his horse was crazy or wild, but that in his vision it danced around in that queer way.

It was this vision that gave him his great power, for when he went into a fight, he had only to think of that world to be in it again, so that he could go through anything and not be hurt. Until he was killed at the Soldiers' Town on White River, he was wounded only twice, once by accident and both times by some one of his own people when he was not expecting trouble and was not thinking; never by an enemy."

This story appears to be an addition by John G. Neihardt, as his original interview transcripts with Black Elk make no mention of the origination of Crazy Horse's name.

Crazy Horse received a black stone from a medicine man named Horn Chips to protect his horse, a black-and-white "paint" which he named Inyan (rock or stone). He placed the stone behind the horse's ear, so that the medicine from his vision quest and Horn Chips would combine; he and his horse would be one in battle.

(from Wikipedia via Native American Encyclopedia, used by Creative Commons Attribution/Share-Alike License 3.0)

❖

NO TEARS, JUST QUIET REFLECTION
Linda Amos-Ganther

No tears, just quiet reflection,
Filled my body and my soul,
As I, alone, knelt in this empty kirkyard,
By the grave marker that bore your name.

No tears, just quiet reflection,
As I recalled all of the tears
I had shed upon learning
The unexpected news of your death,
So very long ago.

No tears, just quiet reflection,
As I admitted that you weren't here,
That you had gone on to "a better place,"
Where neither tears nor hurts
Are allowed to enter in.

NAMING WATER
Carol Willette Bachofner

Gwantigok, Penawahpskek,
Passamaquoddy, Pashipakokee,
long rivers, long through the land you flow
long through us will you flow,
flowing from where the rocks widen,
from where pollack feed us.

Piscataqua, Androscoggin, Cobbosseecontee,
Olamantegok, Quahog,
where water lies between the hills
through the sheltering place,
to where sturgeon gather together
to red ochre river, color of our children.
Shellfish place, treaty-making place.

Sebastcook, Seninebik,
Skowhegan, Baskahegan,
our stories flow
through little channels,
bearing rocks and memories
from where salmon leap the falls
to broad open waters,

turning back to where wild onions grow,
with birch and ash along their backs,
long rivers of first light
through our families flowing:
Wazwtegok, Winoztegok,
Zawakwtegw, Gwantigok.

Ndakinna.

*All place names are from the Abenaki language
❖

THE MOTHER OF ALL OF THE PEOPLE
Okanagon Legend (source unknown)

Old-One, or Chief, made the Earth out of a woman, and she said she would be the mother of all of the people. Thus the earth was once a human being, and she is alive yet; but she has been transformed, and we cannot see her in the same way we can see a person. Nevertheless, she has legs, arms, head, heart, flesh, bones, and blood.

The soil is her flesh; the trees and vegetation are her hair; the rocks, her bones; and the wind is her breath.

She lies spread out, and we live on her. She shivers and contracts when cold, and expands and perspires when hot. When she moves, we have an earthquake. Old-One, after transforming her, took some of the flesh and rolled it into balls, as people do with mud or clay. These he transformed into the beings of the ancient world.

NATIVE AMERICAN DREAMER

V J Schultz

Today, Two Feathers, aka Sam Smith, looked toward the past and turned his back on the plain white-bread future planned for him by his parents. To prove it he posed in full dance costume in front of the eager photographer.

Digging deep, he tried to feel his tribal roots. But all he got was the burning of the hot sun and the tickle of sweat beading down his spine. The Cherokee dance costume covered almost as much, perhaps more, as the business suit he normally wore as a real estate agent.

He snorted, thinking about his job and how it related to where he stood. How ironic that he earned his living from helping people buy and sell land which surely was once tricked or taken from Native Americans.

His enjoyment came not from his work, but from his passion.

Sam Two Feathers enjoyed learning and performing the traditional dances. All the tourist spectators at the intertribal Powwow loved watching him do the grass dance. He came first in the line, preparing the 'dance floor' by flattening the grass underfoot with the precise placement of his feet to the drumming.

And he loved the attention of admirers like the magazine photographer who directed his movements now.

"Great shot," the photographer said. "Stand a bit taller and raise your right hand two more inches. Chin to your left a bit."

Sam Two Feathers drew in more air and puffed out his chest.

"Perfect, that's it."

In the group gathered around the shoot, one petite blonde of obvious Nordic European lineage sent an admiring glance Sam's way before snapping his picture with her phone's camera. She wore her hair long and braided with feathers at the ends.

He shook his head. Powwows, like today, drew out real tribal members and fake wish-they-weres like her who rightly or wrongly claimed a speck of Indian ancestry in a distant past.

Perhaps it was easier for Sam Two Feathers, himself, to believe in his own Native American heritage because he grew up in Springfield, which was a stopping place on the Trail of Tears. He always figured a great-great someone was a Trail of Tears' dropout, staying behind to marry into the local settlers.

Many of those who really did have Native American blood didn't know because, way back when being Native American wasn't trendy, some Cherokees elected to blend with settlers. Successful ones of them never spoke of their real origin, thus escaping the stigma and persecution of that dark time in American history.

The chatter of tourists blended with the clicking of the camera.

"Good. Good."

For a moment, he closed his eyes to imagine himself truly back in the past when the land belonged to his people -- the Real People -- and not the European intruders.

Sam Two Feathers knew down deep his family hung upon the Cherokee tribal tree. He hated it that he didn't have proof. His blue eyes and red-brown hair didn't help matters, nor did his freckled skin. His soul felt pure Cherokee.

"Now show me some of the dance moves."

As directed, Sam Two Feathers opened his eyes, lifted his feet and brought them down just so in an ancient pattern.

"Got it. Great shoot."

The camera stilled, but the voices of the drums spoke louder now. He nodded at the photographer and kept his feet moving as he danced toward the Powwow dance circle.

A boy darted out in front of him, mimicking his careful movements. Sam Two Feathers clucked his tongue. Why didn't parents keep a close watch on their kids? Still, he remembered his own excitement when he first saw the dancing. Look where it had led him.

When his parents had stopped at a Powwow on one vacation trip, eight-year old Sam knew then where he belonged. The drums' voices beat in his blood and his feet moved him to dance. Mesmerized, he started to join the line of dancers moving into the circle.

"Get back here!" Dad yanked on his arm and pulled him to where Mom waited.

"What is the matter with you?" she said.

Dragging Sam along, they retreated to their Ford station wagon. In moments, they returned to driving down Route 66. Sam sat in the back of the car staring out the back window as the Powwow faded out of sight.

Sam's heart continued beating in time to the drums and the sound; the feeling of belonging never left him over the years. Eight-year old Sam grew up; on the way, he learned more about being Native American and Cherokee.

Two Feathers became his Native American name; he picked it because he liked the sound. Not because it was a traditional Cherokee name.

"Jeff, get out of the dancer's way."

Sam blinked back to the present and looked toward the woman who spoke. She was the blonde with the braids; the make-believe Native American.

"I'm just dancing," the boy said.

"Dance right over here." She held out her hand to the child who made a face.

Despite the protesting expression, the boy did as told.

As Sam Two Feathers kept in step to the beat, the boy continued to dance along anchored to the woman's side. All though his performance, Sam Two Feathers caught glimpses of the two outside the dance area. It was a bit disconcerting because the boy mirrored each of his movements.

When finished, Sam Two Feathers started to leave the dance circle.

"Hey, mister! Will you teach me to dance like you?"

Sam Two Feathers stopped short of running into the boy who had jumped in front of him as he spoke.

"Jeff Barnard, what are you doing?" The blonde glared at the boy.

"It's okay," Sam Two Feathers said.

He watched her raise her gaze to meet his eyes.

"Sorry about my brother."

Despite himself, he felt drawn to her. "I had the same curiosity when I was his age."

"We really aren't Indian. He probably shouldn't learn the dance."

Those words dug into Sam Two Feathers' heart. He remembered something he had forgotten.

Almost as soon as young Sam's family returned home from their vacation, he ran to make sure the backyard and his toys remained the same as when they had left. Soon he swung high on the swing, peering over the wooden fence into the neighbor's yard.

A familiar figure moved there. Not Mr. Williams, the mean man who always chased him out of the front yard. Did the dancer from the Powwow practice his steps in the backyard next door to his own house?

Sam fell out of the swing and for a moment couldn't breathe.

"Boy, you okay?" An old, old man stood over him. The sun behind the man's head glowed in a halo and outlined the Native American clothes and the feather decorations.

With a loud gasp, Sam drew in air. When he managed to speak, he said, "Who are you--how did you get here?"

The Dancer pursed his lips and looked wise. "I go where the Great Spirit sends me. Today I am here. You have the soul of a grass dancer. You will learn."

A touch on Sam Two Feathers' arm brought him back to the present and the pretty blonde and the boy.

"Are you okay?" she said.

"Never better." He smiled at her. "Your brother has the heart of a Native American like I do."

Sam Two Feathers squatted by Jeff. "As someone once said to me, you have the soul of a grass dancer. You will learn. I did."

WARRIOR'S SONG
Renee Meador

Stand still, you steed, while I get on.
(Did I hear a Warrior's song?)

The gate is closed; the hill is steep.
Stand still, dear horse. Don't move your feet.
The prancing hoof unearths a stone,
A fist-sized terra cotta stone
Containing such a reddish hue
Before I picked it up, I knew.

The chert is cool in my hand.
The ridges sharp by man's command.
An artisan of years gone by
Shaped this tool with skillful eye
To fit the palm, to scrape the hide,
Or on the war club to be tied.

Ere fence and gate crisscrossed this land
There came a roving Blackfoot band,
Their ponies thundering o'er the rise
Beneath the bluff before my eyes.

They galloped to this very place
Where pines rise from hillside's face,
Traversed the hill beside the pines
Above the stream that softly winds
Below where I now stand,
The Blackfoot brave's chert in my hand.

What caused the chert to fall away?
Did pony falter on that day
As comrades crowded into line
To gallop down the steep incline?
Perhaps a pony here was lost,
The cannon snapped; the rider tossed.

The lament of that Blackfoot brave
Heard now in wind through barren crags.
The chert worked by the Blackfoot brave
Through tens of winters here has lain
Until today by merest chance
My mount upon the earth did dance.

Stand still, you steed, while I get on.
Do *you* hear the Warrior's song?

REDEEM THE TRUTH
Harold E. Grice

Redeem the truth from the mind of ideas

Let the words that come have meaning

To reach a sense of awareness

That guides to being real

"Ask questions from you heart and
you will be answered from the heart."
~ *Native American Proverb ~ Omaha*

WARRIORS OF THE RAINBOW

There would come a time when the Earth would be ravaged of its resources, the sea blackened, the streams poisoned, and the deer dropping dead in their tracks.

Just before it was too late, the Indian would regain his spirit and teach the white man reverence for the Earth, banding together with him to become Warriors of the Rainbow.

There was an old lady, from the Cree tribe, named "Eyes of Fire", who prophesied that one day, because of the white man's' or Yo-ne-gi's greed, there would come a time, when the fish would die in the streams, the birds would fall from the air, the waters would be blackened, and the trees would no longer be, mankind as we would know it would all but cease to exist.

There would come a time when the "keepers of the legend, stories, culture rituals, and myths, and all the Ancient Tribal Customs" would be needed to restore us to health. They would be mankind's' key to survival, they were the "Warriors of the Rainbow". There would come a day of awakening when all the peoples of all the tribes would form a New World of Justice, Peace, Freedom and recognition of the Great Spirit.

The "Warriors of the Rainbow" would spread these messages and teach all peoples of the Earth or "Elohi". They would teach them how to live the "Way of the Great Spirit".

They would tell them of how the world today has turned away from the Great Spirit and that is why our Earth is "Sick".

The "Warriors of the Rainbow" would show the people that this "Ancient Being" (the Great Spirit) is full of love and understanding, and teach them how to make Earth (Elohi) beautiful again. These Warriors would give the people principles or rules to follow to make their path right with the world. These principles would be those of the

Ancient Tribes. The Warriors of the Rainbow would teach the people of the ancient practices of Unity, Love and Understanding.

They would teach of Harmony among people in all four corners of the Earth.

Like the Ancient Tribes, they would teach the peoples how to pray to the Great Spirit with love that flows like the beautiful mountain stream, and flows along the path to the ocean of life. Once again, they would be able to feel joy in solitude and in councils. They would be free of petty jealousies and love all mankind as their brothers, regardless of color, race or religion. They would feel happiness enter their hearts, and become as one with the entire human race.

Their hearts would be pure and radiate warmth, understanding and respect for all mankind, Nature, and the Great Spirit. They would once again fill their minds, hearts, souls, and deeds with the purest of thoughts. They would seek the beauty of the Master of Life – the Great Spirit! They would find strength and beauty in prayer and the solitudes of life.

Their children would once again be able to run free and enjoy the treasures of Nature and Mother Earth. Free from the fears of toxins and destruction, wrought by the Yo-ne-gi and his practices of greed. The rivers would again run clear, the forests abundant and beautiful, the animals and birds would be replenished. The powers of the plants and animals would again be respected and conservation of all that is beautiful would become a way of life.

The poor, sick and needy would be cared for by their brothers and sisters of the Earth. These practices would again become a part of their daily lives.

Photo from "Native Americans: Photos from the Public Domain" (Facebook Page)

The leaders of the people would be chosen in the old way – not by their political party, or who could speak the loudest, boast the most, or by name calling or mudslinging, but by those whose actions spoke the loudest. Those who demonstrated their love, wisdom, and courage and those who showed that they could and did work for the good of all, would be chosen as the leaders or Chiefs.

They would be chosen by their "quality" and not the amount of money they had obtained. Like the thoughtful and devoted "Ancient Chiefs", they would understand the people with love, and see that their young were educated with the love and wisdom of their surroundings. They would show them that miracles can be accomplished to heal this world of its ills, and restore it to health and beauty.

The tasks of these "Warriors of the Rainbow" are many and great. There will be terrifying mountains of ignorance to conquer and they shall find prejudice and hatred. They must be dedicated, unwavering in their strength, and strong of heart. They will find willing hearts and minds that will follow them on this road of returning "Mother Earth" to beauty and plenty – once more.

The day will come, it is not far away. The day that we shall see how we owe our very existence to the people of all tribes that have maintained their culture and heritage, those that have kept the rituals, stories, legends, and myths alive. It will be with this knowledge, the knowledge that they have preserved, that we shall once again return to "harmony" with Nature, Mother Earth, and mankind. It will be with this knowledge that we shall find our "Key to our Survival".

This is the story of the "Warriors of the Rainbow" and this is my reason for protecting the culture, heritage, and knowledge of my ancestors. I know that the day "Eyes of Fire" spoke of – will come! I want my children and grandchildren to be prepared to accept this task. The task of being one of the........ "Warriors of the Rainbow."

From Native American Encyclopedia, used via Creative Commons Attribution/Share-Alike License 3.0 (Source: firstpeople) ❖

POW WOW TIME

Judy Olson Mosca

He stands tall and proud
against the mystical evening sky
dressed in his wacipi regalia.

He dances with pride
his eagle feathers soaring with grace
with every step and beat
of the host drums

honoring his ancestors before him
honoring the elders to the tiny tots
all dances, vendors, attendees
honoring all creation
with the dance.

The wacipi brings out the beauty
of the land, the people, the culture.

All people are welcome
they come
they dance
they watch
and listen to the drum
the heart beat
of us all.

Mitakuye Oyasin.
We are all related.

DISSIPATING VISION
Cindy Bechtold

Sand slides over the backs of her hands
as she sinks them deep into the creek.
Eddies spin tubs of lapping soap –
frothing invitations.

Unbraiding her hair, she
lifts foamy handfuls to lather,
rinse in a still spot – moss astride
stones warmed under streaked sun.

Pony hooves shift in a grove nearby.
Smoke scoots overhead as venison sears.
I breathe in shallow sighs, willing her to stay.
May I, a hurried woman of today, join her there?

She lies on her side, plucking snake grass,
pulling it apart at the rings, tubes that
will never fit tightly again. Setting
the pieces aside, she returns to the water's

edge, scooping handfuls of bubbles,
blowing them across the way.

SHADOW, MY DREAM GUIDE

Yvonne Londres, aka Dances with Poetry

He came in a strong black shadow of Native American image,
leaping into a sudden nap, following my exhaustive searching and
 crying
where he helped lead tears into inspired sleep.

I wept because my great-great-grandmother's words seemed lost
 forever,
a language that once flowed as often as mighty rivers.
Those were the words my soul needed to know for claiming my
 heritage.

"You have always loved the spirit echo," Shadow, the dream guide
 spoke.
"For he has recorded and retold the first Native infant's cry,
plus every utterance and whisper that followed.

"By dream you can follow me to the towering amethyst mountains,
where the echo's spirit lives, replies, and has stored all verbal
 communications.
The older the language, the closer to the echo heart it rests.

"There, in the jagged risen masses of stone, you can see the
 opening.
Are you brave enough to go through it with me?
We can gather up the words as blossoms of expressions,
placing them into your great-great-grandmother's hand woven
 baskets."

Courageously, I follow through the echoing time portal.
I awake fluently speaking my true *Siletz Dee-ni* language.

WHITE MAN TEACHER
Houstine Cooper

He comes to teach us.
We must learn the words and ways of
the white man, the elders told us.
"Our parents teach us words. Braves
show us how to hunt and fish in
the forest and streams the Great Spirit
has given us so we can live free.
We don't need him," we children said.

But still he came.

He lived among us. Played our games
and called each of us by name.
He cared about us and our concerns.
He told us stories to help us
learn our words correctly.
We learned from him.
He learned from us.

He built our school.

Then taught us respect for
it as a house of worship
as well as the place
to learn from books.
He helped us into manhood.
We missed him
when he went away.

To marry his sweetheart, he said.

His teachings were good.
He helped us to understand. We then taught
our children his ways along with ours.
Many of our children have moved from our
village in the forest. They remember
their ancestors but have adopted the
ways of the white man.

The white man teacher was wise.

"What is life? It is the flash of a firefly in the night.
It is the breath of a buffalo in the wintertime.
It is the little shadow which runs across the
grass and loses itself in the sunset."
~ *Native American Proverb ~ Blackfoot*

THE BEGINNING OF TIME

The Great Spirit became lonely and took a seed from his pocket and held it between his hands and blew his warm breath on it and our world began to form. As it grew he added a pinch of sage to his hands and it became the land. While sitting there all alone he cried a tear and it became the waters. As he looked at his creation he knew it would need a caretaker, so he tossed it into the air and blew the winds across it to hold it in place. He took a piece of cedar and tossed it on to his new world and it became the animals.

Seeing all this was good he reached into his pocket and withdrew the blue-corn meal and tossed it onto the world and it became the grasses and plants.

The next day he entered this new world and named all the animals: The Four-Legs, The Winged Ones, and those that swam in the waters. Looking around he came to understand there were no Two-Legged ones so he reached down and took a hand full of earth and blew on it and it was the first human being.

This is how my grandmother told me about the coming of our world.

Story from Native American Encyclopedia, used via Creative Commons Attribution/ Share-Alike License 3.0 (Source: littlewolfrun) Image from Inspired Graphics.

FLIGHT OF THE FIN AND FEATHER
Barbara Callahan Quin

Fish
have fins
Birds have wings
Fish blow bubbles
while feathered Bird sings
Legend says that the Birds were Fish before
but they were Fish who longed to soar,
caught beneath their watery world,
God smiled on their Fish-Hearts
and gave them Wings

AHIGA'S QUEST
Madeline McEwen

The light failed, but Ahiga forged onwards through the undergrowth in the gloom, keeping close to the shadows cast by the tree line. At home, Leotie--Flower of the Prairie--waited for him, delirious, the fever raging through her body. He must get home with the medicine, if not to save her, at least to hold her hand one last time before life slipped away.

The journey back home to Two Rivers Creek took far longer on foot. His hair was plastered to his back and shoulders, drenched from the fine wet mist permeating the heavy air. He had dressed with care for the meeting with the white man, John Thornton. Now, more than a day later, Ahiga's breechcloth and leggings were mud-stained and damp. His chosen headdress, a simple band of hide with a hawk and owl feather bound together auspiciously to represent life, renewed his hope. He watched the sun dip behind the mountains and knew another day was lost. How long would Leotie survive the torment of the sickness?

All the remedies they had tried had failed. None of the traditional ways had any effect. This new and lethal sickness had slashed and slain his kinsmen. It cut down a victim, racking the body with fever and chills. It attacked the young and the old, the weak and the strong, without favor or pity. And that cough, straining to escape, like thunder from a frail ribcage of bones, draining the body of power.

Ahiga could still hear in his thoughts the hacking coughs from the others in the longhouse back home. They sounded like the calls of a mysterious bird, an invader who came to steal the breath away from every living being. The cough began in a low tone deep in the dark cavities of a body, the sound modulating and rising high, followed by the victims gasping to recover their breath. Then, barely minutes later, another onslaught brought them down, the coughs whooping through the longhouse and echoing far out to hang in the still mountain air.

Paralyzed with fear and frustration, Ahiga had to act, had to escape. He went in search of a man called John Thornton. It was said Thornton had a cure, but Ahiga had to travel alone. He was one of the few who were young, remaining strong and fit, leaving the others to care for the sick. Men and women worked together fulfilling their role for the wellness of the whole. Why had he been spared? The sickness lasted for several weeks, but there was no way to tell who would survive and who would succumb.

Never before had he traveled so far, except when he was a boy. Then he went with his father and four other kinsmen, one of whom spoke the settlers' language. Together, they had ridden to a settlement to trade during the harsh winter when local suppliers were low.

This time, he had taken a new direction, to the south where Thornton treated the sick. It was said that he would sell to anyone and Ahiga had found this to be true.

Again, Ahiga cursed his stupidity, riding too fast, not allowing his horse Nikita to rest, too anxious and foolish to yield to natural fatigue. Now Ahiga paid the price. He had treated the gash in his leg with a poultice bound by reeds after Nikita floundered and threw him against a rocky outcrop.

First, he had assessed Nikita's foreleg. The whites of her eyes bulged from her sweet face. She whinnied in pain, terror, and exhaustion. Maybe if they had been back home in Two Rivers Creek, he could have saved her. A horse rarely survived a severe break, but occasionally, with splints, prayer, and herbs, the ligaments could be encouraged to mend. Why could he not do this for Nikita, too? Give her the chance of continued life, not as a service to riders, no longer racing sleek and fast over the plains, but maybe as companion.

He knew his thinking was weak. There was no room for the lame, but the thought of losing Nikita caused such pain. There were no choices on the trail. Even if he tied her up to return later, there was little hope of recovery. He might as well kill her now, cleanly, instead of leaving her tethered like a sacrificial offering for any passing pack of savage scavengers. He cleared his mind of Nikita and focused on his quest. Still, he had doubts.

When he had stood before Thornton, Ahiga wished for some of the legendary "Invisible Warriors" skills, like the power to hear all his enemies' war plans. Did Thornton offer truth? Could quinine cure her? Heal Leotie? If only he could use the Invisible Warriors trick to identify liars.

Initially, Ahiga felt little pain, but as the hours wore on and the distance stretched ahead, he found himself limping. He hacked off a branch to act as a walking stick, stripping the limb of twigs and leaves, exposing the smooth pale wood. He cut off a few handfuls of dried grass to use as padding for the forked end and bound it in place with shreds of bison hide from his pack. He tucked this into his armpit after sheathing his knife and set off once again.

Around him, he heard the familiar sounds of the forest, deer grazing and the almost silent steps of their stalkers, but Ahiga smelled their musky scent on the breeze moving the air and sweeping the mist downwind. His fingers smoothed the dark green algae on the thick barked trees in this lonely corridor carrying him away from the settlement and back to the land of his people. He kept moving north at a steady pace, not as quickly as earlier in the day for now his body felt weary and his stomach empty.

So many had already died, and still others fell to the sickness. He unwrapped the cloth protecting the small brown bottle again and checked the cork in the neck for leakage. It was still snug and dry. When he had felt the horse lurch beneath him as she began to fall, Ahiga's first thought was not of his own safety, nor that of Nikita. The only thing on his mind was the survival of the medicine bottle with its promise of healing.

Thornton called it quinine and Ahiga traded twelve of his best hides in exchange for this one small bottle. He would have traded more if needed, a whole season's labor if the remedy worked. But would it? What if he were too late? His journey now moved into the third moon.

Thornton had told Ahiga to leave the longhouse and take Leotie to a smaller dwelling. There Ahiga should fill the shelter with the steam of boiling water to calm the lungs and ease the cough. But Ahiga didn't fully trust this man. Better to remain safely together in the longhouse where they all shared the burden of healing the many sick. There, the songs of the elders and the chants of the wise could fall upon them all.

Why had the sickness picked Leotie? Why not choose his single body rather than hers, she who was with child, soon to birth their firstborn? He thought over the many things he had failed to do. Was this the spirits' revenge? Ahiga knew he had not been diligent. Did his lack of respect bring this cursed sickness upon his loved ones? Watching his family and friends flounder, he felt impotent. It was crueler than experiencing the fever himself, yet he had only himself to blame.

The pain of seeing Leotie struggle, knowing the poison in her blood flowed through their unborn child, two lives threatened instead of his own made him pray they would be spared. Would the spirits relent and allow him to make amends?

Ahiga ate berries sparingly from the pouch tied at his waist. He had taken only three days' supply and had no time to scavenge. Nothing must slow him down. He remembered tempting Leotie with dessert of Buffalo-berries and honey to ease the fevers.

After days of sickness, she had grown so thin the skin on her belly was taut across the infant within. He thought of the tea he made for her from the Red-Clover flowers and how she sipped it through her softly parted lips, how her hand shook, how he placed his hands around hers to steady it and help purify her blood. His efforts made no difference and his patience waned. He knew she was slipping away from him.

Leotie's gentle words of encouragement flooded back to his mind, her unwavering faith in his abilities, and her trust in his nobility. He had always known this woman was to be his. Although he had chosen her, Leotie said that she had chosen him, like the maiden and the Invisible Warrior. In that legend, only the youngest sister could see the truth and did not lie. Like her, Leotie's faith gave him the strength to carry on.

Ahiga drew closer to the mountains, the trees thinning and low lying brush spreading out before him. His throat felt dry. His leg began to throb. He knew he should wait until first light in the morning before trying to cross their treacherous heights. Rest now and wake with a stronger body. Find a cave or shelter, build a fire, eat, and plan his route, but he couldn't lose any more time. He watched thunderous clouds looming over the peaks, threatening to open and drown him with their icy rain, making the granite stone faces of the mountain slick with deception.

The night was cold. Ahiga felt the heat of his own blood coursing through his veins from the strenuous pace of travel. At a creek, he paused to refill his water pouch. His moccasin boots sank into the soft sand. The water was cool and fresh. Cupping his hands, he brought the water to his face and tasted the sweet brackish wetness. He would not stop again until he reached the flat open plains on the other side.

Taking a deep breath, Ahiga strode forward. His fingers searched for secure holds. He negotiated every step, knowing that any wrong move might be his last. He rose higher and higher. The wind grew ever colder, seeping through to his stiff muscles and icy bones, but he kept moving. To stop might prove fatal. Everyone was relying on him. He had to make it through. If only he had started earlier, stopped less frequently, maintained his pace and not surrendered to his own physical needs.

Passing the summit, he looked down. Surely, this passage would prove easier. He had to force himself to hold back as the momentum of the steep gradient lured him to listlessness. He set his teeth and made sure every footfall met the ground firmly. He longed to allow his body to fall, to let his arms spread wide and soar like the mighty eagle on the swirling winds. Light-headed, he stumbled on, step after painful step.

Finally, on reaching the open plain, Ahiga fell to his knees and slumped over onto his side, short of breath. His leg ached as if the bindings had changed into a red-hot tourniquet. His swollen skin felt puffy to the touch. He laid his head on the crook of his arm and rested his eyes. The dawn's light crept over him as he fell into a deep slumber.

Ahiga awoke with a start. The sun was high in the sky. He struggled to stand, dragging his leg, stiff as a poker, hotter than burning embers from a raging bonfire. He scanned the horizon in the hope of spying one of his people out hunting, although this seemed unlikely. Everyone was needed at the longhouse. They would be reliant on stored grain during this terrible period with no time to spend on the laborious work of trapping and hunting.

Just then, by chance, he saw a rider in the distance, or rather the plume of dust in his wake. Ahiga lifted his hands to his mouth and called. The dust trail grew larger until finally Ahiga recognized his youthful friend, Helaku--Sunny Day--as he drew closer, his raised arm punching the air. He pulled his horse to a halt and slipped from his back with light steps. A huge smile of welcome broke upon his face.

Ahiga smiled back with relief and explained what had happened. Helaku examined Ahiga's leg with a grief-stricken expression. Clearly, his wound was worse than Ahiga feared. Helaku helped him mount the horse and then climbed on behind him, reaching forward to hold the reins and support his friend's flagging body.

Together, they traveled at a gentle trot, but Ahiga urged the horse on, clicking his tongue, ignoring Helaku's advice. Ahiga had to get back. He wanted to ask about Leotie, but any words were lost, drowned out by the pounding hooves as they raced across the plain.

When the longhouse came into view through the clearing, Ahiga thought his heart would explode with anticipation. Several kinsmen were waiting, not many, alerted by Helaku's warning calls. They looked weary, but their tiredness quickly turned to concern when Ahiga slithered from the horse. Someone brought a light stretcher and together they carried Ahiga, others running ahead to make preparations. Ahiga clutched the medicine bottle to his chest.

"Take me to Leotie," he called. "Where is she? How is she? What about the baby?"

No one answered his questions. Instead, they bore him away, not to the longhouse, but to the storage barn behind. There, they pulled the flap open. Ahiga protested. "Take me to Leotie."

"She is here," said an older woman, holding the flap open and beckoning them inside.

A fire burned at the center of the barn. Above, the roof had been modified so a hole allowed the smoke to escape. Where were all the supplies stored now? He tried to adjust his vision to the gloom. He saw several beds. Each one was draped with furs and hides to form separate partitions. He heard the familiar coughs whooping through the muffled enclosures.

They carried him to the far corner where he saw Leotie on a low settle. She had grown even thinner, more fragile than the fluff of duck down. Her dark eyes were red-rimmed as if she had cried every sorrow known to mankind.

"Leotie," he cried.

Ahiga's carriers lowered the stretcher to the ground next to Leotie.

She reached out her hand to his and he let the bottle fall.

"I am so happy to see you," she said, a smile spreading across her face.

Ahiga could find no words of reply. He clung to her hand.

"I am weak," she said, "but I grow strong again."

Ahiga found laughter bubbling up within him. How could this skin and bone woman claim to be well?

"The cough has gone," she said, "and so has the fever. I am one of the lucky."

"Lucky," Ahiga scoffed. "How can this be luck? This is a curse."

"You are wrong," she said. "The spirits are generous to us."

"This is not generosity."

Leotie reached behind her and lifted a small swaddled bundle. She parted the thick, soft blanket, making the opening wider and revealing the smallest, sweetest face he had ever seen.

"What name do you choose for our daughter?" Leotie said, pressing the child into his arms.

"Heavy," he said marveling at the robust baby.

"What kind of a name is that?" Leotie said, giggling.

"A name that will live longer than either of us," he said. "A healthy girl, more solid than stone, more beautiful than a golden harvest, and more precious than the sacred water of life."

(public domain image from www.pdclipart.org)

THE SACRED EARTH

"Every part of the earth is sacred to my people.
Every shining pine needle, every sandy shore, every
mist in the dark woods, every meadow, every humming
insect. All are holy in the memory and experience of my
people."

—*Chief Seattle, Suquamish and Duwamish*
(Chief Seattle's image from Wikimedia Commons)

The role of legend

as an educational tool for teaching Indian children survival skills is reflected in this powerful poem by William Childress, 80, of Folsom, California. Childress is a Pulitzer-nominated writer and poet, Korean War veteran, and ex-paratrooper. As a white boy growing up in Arizona, he played with Apache children on the San Carlos Apache Indian Reservation, at the time one of the poorest Indian reservations in America. The poem describes one of his childhood adventures. Gila monsters are poisonous, but too slow-moving to be dangerous.

No deaths by Gila monster bite have been recorded, but the bite is excruciating. Their venom is now being mined for cancer and Alzheimer's drugs. Gilas are endangered and protected.

In frontier days, Gilas sometime reached twenty-seven inches and thirty-five pounds. About fourteen inches is the norm today as habitat encroachment reduces food supplies.

Wanda Sue Parrott discovered this poem by William Childress among entries in the 2013 Senior Poets Laureate Poetry Competition for American poets age 50 and older. Since Native American wisdom based on legend was the inspiration for the piece, she shared the poem with *Legends* editor Barbara Callahan Quin, who contacted Childress for permission to use it in this volume. He said yes.

In an e-mail to Wanda, Childress said:

I could not have any poem that I'd rather you liked... it's a favorite of mine, too, and is based on an actual incident at Coolidge Dam, in Arizona in the 1940s. I had crawled into this fissure during a rain shower and when I finally looked behind me, I saw I was in a whole nest of Gilas. I quickly chose the rain as better company. They're beautiful, though, especially after being washed by a rain."

See NEXT PAGE...

IN THE GILA MONSTER DEN
by William Childress

The Gila Monster is North America's
only poisonous lizard. When it bites,
it hangs on, chewing its poison in.

In the Arizona summer,
it hisses across the lake,
a desert rainstorm
beading the water's skin.

A narrow crevice
cuts the cliff above me.
On all fours, like a lizard,

I squirm into its dryness,
a saurian eons removed
from the timeless rocks

that protect me.
Then I see my brothers.
With eyes like wet black pebbles

they slither toward me,
their claws knifing the dust.
I wait in my cold white skin

as the leader moves to confront them,
massive, slow and all powerful
in his little crease of the world,

and though I am filled with terror,
I marvel at the beauty of death,
wrapped in a beaded orange blanket,
mouth closed on his famous smile.

MY MOUSE
Doreen Lindahl

On a brown furrow of newly plowed earth
sat a mouse.
Quick as a snatch, he was in my hands,
    soft and warm and wiggly.

I got a box for his house and
wheat from the granary
    so he wouldn't have to look for food.

He wouldn't eat and he wouldn't squeak,
so I held him and took him for a walk.
    I loved him so.

Down by the chicken house,
the little mouse bit my finger.
In pain, my hands opened and my mouse
    dangled from its tooth-hold on my finger.
With a wild snap of my hand,
    he flew off into the tall grass.

I loved him... but he bit me.

It was many years before I realized that
love gives freedom,
    not confining dependency.

Love is holding in the heart,
    not imprisonment in the hand.
That was why my little mouse didn't squeak...
    he was too unhappy to talk.

How could he realize
I was too young to know
how to love him
    more than I loved
        loving him?

REFLECTIONS ON A SILHOUETTE:
GREAT SPIRITS LIVE ON
Vincent J. Tomeo

Your silhouette against the rising sun and parting clouds speaks to one, like Easter, a new day, timeless and immortal. Yet, your headdress is carried on your back and not worn on your head. Why is this? Are you resigned to your fate? Is that why your hands are at your sides? Yet, you stand as if in pride as you walk into infinity with your back against the sun.

Do you feel lost in this present world? What would one say to you if we met on the Great Plains? Oh, noble warrior, we are sorry! Proud brave walking out of the clouds, you now stand like a Corinthian Column saluting the sky. Will you dance to the gods of nature? Will your message be heard? Do you stand and moan the plight of earth? Is your spirit haunted? Will you roam the land for eternity? Can you not rest? Will your legends live on? Do you hear the call of the eagles, the cry of the wolves, the stampede of the buffalo, and the melting of the icebergs? The animals are lost and now crying as they are wandering into the cities, rummaging through the garbage to survive.

Hear the icebergs explode and constantly dripping! The water rising, the storms are erratic and the seasons unpredictable. Do you fear the rape of planet earth? Is your spirit haunted? The bow and arrow replaced by the rifle, the rifle replaced by missiles! The developers are filling in the plains; the immigrants are still coming. Now the white buffalos are gone. Yet, you still stand tall and proud. Will your legend die?

The arrow has pierced your headdress, but is not broken and reflects the rays of the sun. Where is your horse to carry you off into the great winds? Great Spirit! Are you walking out of the clouds? Will we see you in the glaring light? Will we feel your presence? Does anyone hear your drums beating? The treaties were violated and dishonored. The immigrants have moved in. Where has this left you? You have fallen off your horse and have gotten up? Now beat your drums, sing your chants, and recite your poems. Your legends must be heard. Only then, will the great spirits live on. The clouds will part. The sun will glow. The rainbows will cast their colors across the sky, and you will walk with your headdress on.

"Before eating, always take time to thank the food."
~ *Native American Proverb, Arapaho*

BOSS OF THE WILDERNESS
Carol Dee Meeks

You are the yap beneath the moon,
the bay that pierces midnight's light.
Among the stars
in heaven's rug,
you are the howl that rules the wild.
I am the hare who runs to hide
when roars divide the peaceful times
on canyon's rim
and desert floors.
I am afraid to hear your yelps.
We are the native prairie life
as creatures playing hide and seek
when Lobos rule
in loud ado—
with glassy eyes and brazen stance.
Sometimes I hear his mournful song
and watch the critters freeze in fear.
The Lobo mocks,
he jeers and sneers,
to show the wilderness he's boss.

❖

THE FORGOTTEN EAR OF CORN

An Arikara woman was once gathering corn from the field to store away for winter use. She passed from stalk to stalk, tearing off the ears and dropping them into her folded robe. When all was gathered she started to go, when she heard a faint voice, like a child's, weeping and calling:

"Oh, do not leave me! Do not go away without me."

The woman was astonished. "What child can that be?" she asked herself. "What babe can be lost in the cornfield?"

She set down her robe in which she had tied up her corn, and went back to search; but she found nothing.

As she started away she heard the voice again:

"Oh, do not leave me. Do not go away without me."

She searched for a long time. At last in one corner of the field, hidden under the leaves of the stalks, she found one little ear of corn. This it was that had been crying, and this is why all Indian women have since garnered their corn crop very carefully, so that the succulent food product should not even to the last small nubbin be neglected or wasted, and thus displease the Great Mystery

Source: www.indianlegend.com/sioux

LIGHT WARRIOR
Cindy M. Hutchings

An aura   of light
shining white frames
his   silhouette

adorns   his feathered body

back   to blanket
drifting clouds, sweeping
skyline, caressing wind

breath of spirit
Grandfather *blows* by
flattens prairie grass
makes way
for   his dance

the warrior   will step out
give his heart to the drum
heartbeat of earth mother

give all he has to encourage
the people encircling the dance

share the Light that blesses him
with elders, mothers, children,
brother and sister warriors
singers who honor
ancient songs

called to dance
heal hearts, help
people endure, live strong
in

          sacred
                    beauty.

HOW THE FAWN
GOT ITS SPOTS

Long ago, when the world was new, Wakan Tanka, The Great Mystery, was walking around. As he walked he spoke to himself of the many things he had done to help the four-legged ones and the birds survive.

"It is good," Wakan Tanka said. "I have given Mountain Lion sharp claws and Grizzly Bear great strength; it is much easier now for them to survive.

"I have given Wolf sharp teeth and I have given his little brother, Coyote, quick wits; it is much easier now for them to survive.

"I have given Beaver a flat tail and webbed feet to swim beneath the water and teeth which can cut down the trees and I have given slow-moving Porcupine quills to protect itself. Now it is easier for them to survive.

"I have given the Birds their feathers and the ability to fly so that they may escape their enemies. I have given speed to the Deer and the Rabbit so that it will be hard for their enemies to catch them. Truly it is now much easier for them to survive."

However, as Wakan Tanka spoke, a mother Deer came up to him. Behind her was her small Fawn, wobbling on weak new legs.

"Great One," she said. "It is true that you have given many gifts to the four-leggeds and the winged ones to help them survive. It is true that you gave me great speed and now my enemies find it hard to catch me. My speed is a great protection, indeed. But what of my little one here? She does not yet have speed. It is easy for our enemies, with their sharp teeth and their claws, to catch her. If my children do not survive, how can my people live?"

"Wica yaka pelo!" said Wakan Tanka. "You have spoken truly; you are right. Have your little one come here and I will help her."

Then Wakan Tanka made paint from the earth and the plants. He painted spots upon the fawn's body so that when she lays still her color blended in with the earth and she could not be seen. Then Wakan Tanka breathed upon her, taking away her scent.

"Now," Wakan Tanka said, "your little ones will always be safe if they only remain still when they are away from your side. None of your enemies will see your little ones or be able to catch their scent."

So it has been from that day on. When a young deer is too small and weak to run swiftly, it is covered with spots that blend in with the earth. It has no scent and it remains very still and close to the earth when its mother is not by its side. And when it has grown enough to have the speed Wakan Tanka gave its people, and then it loses those spots it once needed to survive.

From Native American Encyclopedia, used via Creative Commons Attribution/Share-Alike License 3.0 (Source: firstpeople)

FORGIVE EVERYONE EVERYTHING

Judy Olson Mosca

On December 10, 2012, American Indians on horseback
started a long cold ride, a 16-day journey
from South Dakota
to Mankato, Minnesota,
site of the mass hanging on December 26, 1862,
of their 38 ancestors
plus two later

A ride of remembrance
and forgiveness
honoring their memory
their courage, songs
and belief the Great Spirit
would catch them
as the gallows fell
150 years ago

2012 – the 150-year anniversary –
the year of reconciliation
remembering the 38-plus-2
with a new scroll with their names

A time of healing
remembering
honoring
coming together

A new slogan, a new hope and dream
"Forgive Everyone Everything"

announced by the Lakota speaker
on a cold day
at the site of the biggest
mass execution
in our country

riding into Mankato
– a town many wouldn't enter –
– until –
Bud Lawrence, a Mankato white man,
and Amos Owen, a Dakota,
met fishing at a stream
and caught a friendship
that changed history in 1958,
creating the Mankato Wacipi – Pow wow
bringing back the American Indians
to their homelands
in the spirit of reconciliation

The wacipi in September
at the Land of Memories Park
brings out the beauty
of the land, the people, the culture

ALL people are welcome
they come
they dance
they watch
and listen to the drum
the heartbeat
of us all

Mitayue Owasin
We are all related

THE LEGEND OF GLISTEN TRAIL
Yvonne Londres, aka Dances with Poetry

It was a moment of extreme wonder and delight for me; I finally realized that my precious pet snail, Glisten Trail, was communicating to me in sign language. She used the long antennae on her head in active guided motions to sign to me. How could I have overlooked her patient, continuing communication efforts for such a long while? Surely, she had been reading my lips with the eyes on the tip-tops of her antennae. She then replied back in a pattern of signed moves using each antennae.

"Glisten Trail, you have saved me from a day of tragic misery," I expressed. "At last, I am recognizing and understanding your signing abilities. This new communication has lightened my spirit, and taken tremendous difficulties from my mind. As you have probably noticed, our tribe has been brutally forced to move onto this bleak and barren reservation. I carried you with me in the soft lining of my dress pocket on this lengthy, undesired journey. Now we have tiredly reached our dismal destination.

"This bleak, barren place is unlike our lush, green former home that we so loved and cherished. Every tribal member grieves deeply because of their imprisonment on this parched property. All now worry about dehydration and starvation on this seemingly lifeless land. My father Chief Strong Elk suffers more than any other. Although he loves his people and continuously tries his best to positively lead them, he feels that he has failed. I have often tried to comfort my wonderful father to no avail. Even lately, I have tried to console him, explaining it is not his fault. The army out numbered and outgunned us in a sudden, unannounced tribal occupation. At gunpoint, we had the choice to quickly move as instructed or be shot to death mercilessly.

"My father tried to speak out courageously against the army general. Father announced that he was the chief and leader of the Cherokee. My father knows English well, and spoke out justly and eloquently, loudly proclaiming our rights, but he was struck down harshly. He fell to the ground in an unconscious state. When Father came to, he was slung over a horse that was being guided by a soldier toward this hot, useless desert area.

"Prior to settlers coming and taking over our residence, Father was a strong chief who walked in the sun with courage, compassion, and confidence. He always tried to help the tribe prosper and advance. One of his greatest achievements was when he discovered a gold mine and gave it to our people. With the gold gathered, we made and sold necklaces, bracelets, and rings. Father traveled to faraway places to sell our creations and fairly divided the money among our tribe. As more settlers intruded into our land, they spied on us to find the location of our gold mine. Then they stole it from us. Afterward, we became impoverished."

I noticed Glisten Trail's small eyes widen. She kept her watch intently on my lips with each word I spoke.

"It has always been so good to talk to you about all the trials, tribulations, and gladness in my life," I uttered honestly. "Things seem especially wondrous now that you can understand my words and sign to me. It does my young, twelve-year-old heart good.

"I became closer to you after my loving mother's recent death from a severe case of pneumonia. Her name was Eyes of Nature. It was such an appropriate name for her: she noticed and enjoyed every form of nature. Truly, she loved snails most, and you, Glisten Trail, were her favorite.

"When the tribe was suffering in poverty, she would say, 'We are never poor when we appreciate and recognize nature's free gifts to us.

Snails glide and create such beauteous oozes that even the sun, moon, and stars spotlight and reflect the sparkling moistness.' Mother complemented the snail's patient, peaceful glide. She used their slow motion as an example for us not to hurry or worry, but to live in peace, contentment, and happiness. Mother was a storyteller. She often entertained and encouraged the tribe with her tales that revolved around the many joys of nature.

"Mother named me Kisses of Snails. I, too, loved the liquid wonder snails spread over the ground; I saw it as snail's kissing the earth. When I first learn to speak, I said, 'Mother, the snails are kissing the earth.' Shortly before my mother passed, she held you, Glisten Trail. Your plump, damp, soft, vulnerable body rested in her right hand. Mother spoke in flattering words about your entire body, as well as the round, speckled tan shell home you carry on your back. She expressed that you were so courageous and helpful to risk your life to bring us glimmers of enjoyable earthly decoration and design. Mother added that you risked being stepped on, unappreciated, rejected, or being eaten by a predator. 'Against all odds, the courage and kindness of the snail never fails,' my mother voiced in appreciation. Many of her last words were prayers for the snails she so admired. She also left my entire family and tribe with uplifting words."

"Try to sleep now, sweet child, Kisses of Snails, for you have yawned numerous times," signed Glisten Trail, the snail. "Let your pretty face rest and relax your oak-bark-shaded eyes. Although you are not yet pleased with this desert, you can still love the heavens above. Perhaps you would find it pleasant to observe the quarter moon as a yellow, illuminated canoe tonight. You may also wish to notice the Orion constellation sparkle with no fog to block the amazing view.

"I hope you dream of your dear mother, as I will certainly recall how she loved, understood, and respected us snails," signed Glisten Trail with her busy moving antennae. "We appreciated how she tried to teach others to enjoy our jewel-like glowing art on the sands. We were grateful that your mother used our slow, patient movements as inspiring messages not to fret, hurry, or lose patience. Just as we snails do, everyone should travel through life in a pleasant, peaceful pace. Relax now, Little One. I think I will have an answer to some of your big survival problems in the morning."

I fell asleep quickly and dreamt of mother standing barefoot on a puffed white cloud with snails swirling decorations about her feet. In the midst of the night, I awakened. I felt distressed because I was not in my comfortable former home. Then I looked up again to Orion's constellation of stars to focus on their beauty, rather than my problems. Changing my thoughts enabled me to drift back to sleep.

Awaking again just before dawn, I worried about little Glisten Trail, the thoughtful snail. She had big dreams to help our people from this overwhelming experience. How could a creature so small believe she could carry out such big feats? Fortunately, I quickly remembered how my mother thought very highly of snails. I rested my eyes again, until I felt the new morning rays of the sun warm my face.

When my eyes opened to the new day, I saw Glisten Trail beside me. She moved her antennae about emphatically and anxiously, trying to give me a signed message that seemed of utmost importance. Before I focused on the language from her antennae, I noticed her snail trail brighter and somewhat thicker in substance. Then I watched as she moved her antennae in vigorous excitement.

"I have the answer to your tribe's most serious problems of survival," she signed boldly.

"How can you help us, Snail of Goodness?" I inquired.

"I vividly recollect the many times your mother praised us, and even used snails as a way to encourage her people through hard times. I love how she enjoyed and appreciated our snail trails, and saw them as beautiful art of glimmering trails over the dirt. You spoke to me of the time your fine father found a gold mine, and gave it to his people to survive. I then realized how important gold is to humans. I questioned why I had always exuded mere pretty gleams of trails. Why not release real golden ones? I wondered as I imagined oozing out rich trails. I tried it, and realized it was easy to release and spread fluid golden gifts over the grounds. Perhaps you have already noticed the extra golden shimmer and thickness I lavished over your new lands. These are genuine wet gold trails. When they dry, you can pick them up and have solid forms of gold to help your tribe survive and prosper.

"I realize your tribe is used to a different form of fertile land, one where you grow delicious fresh vegetables, but this desert could become a great oasis for you. Now you have the gold to purchase water and all the things needed to help this wide area flourish. The good thing about me giving you this gold is that it can never be stolen, or bring about war, or violence. You may enjoy your gold in peace. People searching these desert lands for the origins of your gold will only see me as a common snail spreading slime on the ground. Your people, the Native Americans, adored me. Your family and tribe saw us snails as spreading artistic treasures. Now, your love, gratitude, and positive thoughts toward me have come back to the Cherokee as a good dream coming true."

Just as Glisten Trail, my beloved snail, predicted, we used the snail-given gold to build this desert into an enormous, grand oasis. People have often come on our land to seek out the source of our gold, but they never find it. This tribe now prospers. We have lived in peace for many years. Our people have never been moved from this land because only our tribe, and Glisten Trail, the snail, know the secret of our golden riches. Father is again a glad leader, and walks with pride across to our vast blooming oasis-land.

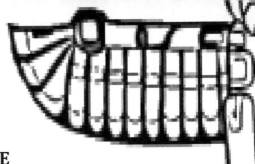

TRAIL OF TIME
Neal "Badger Bob White" Whitman

brothers
living cedar
and storied totem pole
two ravens calling back and forth
deeply carved
living cedar trees
and carved totem poles
stand side by side
as we walk through the grove
ravens echo

TWO WOLVES

THE TWO WOLVES*

One evening, an old Cherokee told his grandson
about a battle that goes on inside people.

He said, "My son, the battle is between two wolves
inside us all. One is Evil. It is anger, envy, jealousy,
sorrow, regret, greed, arrogance, self-pity, guilt,
resentment, inferiority, lies, false pride,
superiority, and ego.

"The other is Good. It is joy, peace, love,
hope, serenity, humility, kindness, benevolence,
generosity, empathy, truth, compassion, and faith."

The grandson thought about this for a minute and
then asked the grandfather, "Which wolf wins?"

The old Cherokee simply replied,
"The one you feed."

❖

*original source unknown, believed to be in Public Domain.
Wolf image on this page from www.all-about-wolves.com, used with site's permission.

...THIS OLD BOULEVARD...
Linda Amos

Her trees...   She'd loved this old boulevard
That her great-great-grandmamma
          Had hand dug and planted in 1863 –
Hopeful for both her beloved husband and her son's
          Victorious ride through to home.

Her trees...   She'd loved this old boulevard
That her great-grandmamma
          Had pruned in fits and plundered
With jealousy and rage against her long gone husband
          During the Spanish-American War.

Her trees...   She loved this old boulevard
That her grandmamma
          Had watered and fed, raked and hoed,
While her husband, a doughboy, wandered throughout
          Europe and Africa in The Great War.

Her trees...   She loved to this old boulevard
That her mama
          Had mulched, pruned, and trimmed,
While her husband had sailed The Pacific Ocean
          Defending American islands against the Japanese.

Her trees...   She loved this old boulevard
That she
          Had tied with hundreds of yellow ribbons
For her beau, the smart young Marine, who never came
home
          But died in the Tet Offensive in Vietnam.

Her trees...   She loved this old boulevard
That her daughter
        Now wrapped with red, white, and blue ribbons
For her young husband, a dapper young Army soldier,
        As she hoped for letters from Afghanistan or Iraq.

Her trees...   She loved this old boulevard
That now sheltered met
        Like a wedding bower o'er those whom she loved best:
Her Father, her husband, her son-in-law;
        Gracing this old house with its beautiful splendor.

Her trees...   She loved this old boulevard
Where she chose to live, love, and grow old.

"It is better to have less thunder in the mouth
and more lightning in the hand."
~ *Native American Proverb ~ Apache*

Native American
Ten Commandments

I. Treat the Earth
and all that dwell
therein with respect.
II. Remain close to
the Great Spirit.
III. Show great respect
for your fellow
beings.
IV. Work together for
the benefit of all
Mankind.
V. Give assistance
and kindness wherever
needed.

Native American
Ten Commandments

VI. Do what you know
to be right.

VII. Look after the
well-being of Mind
and Body.

VIII. Dedicate a
share of your
efforts to the
greater Good.

IX. Be truthful
and honest at
all times.

X. Take full
responsibility
for your actions.

A MOHAWK TALKS
Robert Louis Covington

Many were predestined for my land
the European man claims he found,
a place first scanned and manned by
American Indians already aground.

Oh to have the luxury of going back
in time to that lost garden of delight,
my beginnings, eras of Abram, Noah,
and Tower of Babel, to comprehend—

how ancestry began Great Spirit's
commands to be fertile and multiply,
to pervade the earth and subdue it;

by what way or means Indians first
reached America, taming terrains for
manifold peoples, their mass exits—

from Argentina and Dominica
England, Egypt and Indonesia
Ireland, Japan, and Macedonia
Mexico, Nigeria, Qatar and Russia
Saudi Arabia and Uzbekistan
Zimbabwe, Zambia and other lands—

inciting rightful repine since my kind
were banished to reservations,
now pitched with pacification,
gambling dens defiling humans—

causing regret, because black brother
bought from Africa as human ware
bore many years of brutal slavery,
blatant bigotry here.

Even so, peoples still come; neither
walls, nor laws, nor indigent births
are able to halt Great Spirit's decrees
to be fertile and fill the earth.

I, Native American, and immigrants,
heed the Great Spirit's primal callings,
with gallant toiling, to make my land
a grand nation, ever more evolving.
❖

TWO WORLDS
Martin Willitts Jr.

Always, feet in two worlds, but never belonging in one.
This world is too narrow and sheds me. Where I scatter,
it is not collected here or there. You cannot find what is gone.

I am burning sage brush in a cleansing ceremony. When I split,
I assemble as feverfew. Where I am, I am no more. What I see
is not meant for eyes, nor tongue. My feathers are porcupine quills.

The sun leaves my chest. You ask me who I am, not who I was.
The other world is my breath. My skin dances without moving.
Strawberries grow on my arms in morning chill.

Never one world, when my feet can be in two worlds.
When the scattering ends, the assemblage begins.
My eyesight is traveling geese. What I see is not for me.

When the sun returns to my chest, when the strawberries dance,
when cures are found in plants, I will be there and not there.
What is gone cannot be found. What cannot be spoken is.

BLACK-FOOT
Brenda Bowen

Through rattlesnake weed, a legend unfolds:
Black-footed, feather-father stands brilliant.

Once a Tewa wanderer, now part of the West
with a cloud-croft spirit.

Resilience of a drifter amid the social structures
is the stillness of remembering.

Refuge is the strength in grace,
his vision: the keys of life.

Run past the mystery.
Heroic. Hypnotic. Knight-Errant.

Nomadic into the crossroads... a different world.
Weren't you once that half-breed?

Regardless of acceptance,
not an eagle flies above you.

But there's gold dust now, a private justice.
Somewhere above the city's neon lights,

in a watercolor sky,
a silhouette.

FIRST FRIENDS
Wanda Sue Parrott

When I was young, not yet quite three,
the world was still inside of me;
but shortly before I turned four,
I found it outside our back door.

In Mother's garden, silken strings
were woven by eight-legged things
I heard the universe's sound
among new plants in springtime's ground:

Crisp chirps and chirrs mixed hums of trees
With vocal weed winds, buzz of bees
as sunlight candled shells so frail
I viewed each embryonic snail.

Spiders, ants and slugs were charms
I wore like bracelets on my arms;
my silvereen tattoos were hugs
bestowed in slime ink by young slugs.

Lizards, snakes and geckoes, too,
were friends who shared our backyard zoo,
the universe through which I'd roam
without one step away from home.

I lived in Eden; what is sad
was Mother swore my friends were bad,
and Dad spread poison that would kill
the gentle life forms I love still.

I rescue spiders, flies and worms
and have not yet been killed by germs,
but this is the amazing thing:
I've never yet had one bee sting.

Note: This poem placed #1 Poetry—Jim Stone Grand Prize Memorial
Award, for traditional narrative iambic tetrameter.

VISION QUEST I:

HOW STANDING BEAR GOT HIS NAME
Reprinted with courtesy of Reverend John Buehrens

(Rev. John Buehrens, Past President of the Unitarian Universalist Association, is Interim Minister of the Unitarian Universalist Church of Monterey Peninsula, Carmel, California. Rev. Buehrens presented this story, which he wrote from Lakota history, to the young people at UUCMP in January, 2013. (To learn more about Rev. Buehrens, visit his information page at www.en.wikipedia.org/wiki/John_A._Buehrens.)

This story is called "Vision Quest." It's about a Native American boy called Little Eagle, who had a best friend name Running Bear.

Among their people, the Lakota, a time comes when it is time for boys and girls to leave childhood behind and take up the responsibilities of being a grown-up. These two boys were almost at that age. But one winter an illness came among the people. Many became very sick. Those who had been trading with the white fur traders seemed to get the illness. That included Little Eagle's friend, Running Bear. He became so sick that he died. Little Eagle was very sad.

But soon it was time for Little Eagle and the other youth coming of age to go on a "vision quest." The word for that in Lakota is *Hemblechiya (ham-blay-che-ya)*. It's a word that, taken apart, means "Crying for a Dream."

First, the young people all purified themselves in a sweat lodge.

Then they started to fast, to stop eating. They had to give up every ordinary comfort of living.

Guided by the Medicine Woman, each was then sent to a different place high in the sacred hills, far away from one another and from the valley where the Lakota had made camp for the winter. They were told to focus their minds, their bodies, and their spirits on waiting for a spirit guide – and to stay awake, even at night.

At first that was easy for Little Eagle. The night was very cold, and he was hungry, and feeling very alone, and not a little bit frightened by the sounds he heard – coyotes howling, an owl hooting. And was that the sound of a bear growling? He shivered!

By the second night, Little Eagle felt he couldn't stay awake any longer. His head was spinning. He started to see things that were only in his mind: a warm camp fire, with a cooking pot on it, beyond it, the tepee of his father and mother; then the tepee of Running Bear's family, where he had died.

He started crying. He cried himself to sleep. The vision he had been seeking then came: A young bear was running across a hillside. Then it came to a sudden halt. In Little Eagle's vision the bear grew larger, and then stood up on its hind legs, folded its forepaws, looking straight at him.

When the light of the rising sun startled him awake, he remembered the vision. He made his way back to the camp and to Medicine Woman. She listened to him, then said this:

"The bear that ran is your friend who died. Hold the vision of him standing tall, looking at you. From now on your name is no longer Little Eagle, but Standing Bear. The spirit of your friend has come to you and taught you to be strong, even in the face of death."

Then she sent him into the sweat lodge again, to meditate on what she had said. When he came out she asked if he had the spirit of the bear standing in him, to be strong even before death. When Little Eagle said yes, she announced to the whole people that he was now Standing Bear.

His mother and father now called him by that name. They not only fed him after days of hunger, but gave a great feast in his honor, and dressed him in new clothes, marked with a standing bear.

Medicine Woman told him that his name might never again be changed, but at some point in his life he might want to seek a new vision, and to do yet another vision quest. And so he later did.

But that's another story . . . ❖

VISION QUEST II:

MY ENCOUNTER WITH
FIVE TALL NATIVE AMERICANS
A True Lesson from the Book of Life

Wanda Sue Parrott, aka Prairie Flower

(Following is a report from Wanda Sue Parrott to a colleague in November 2005 about a dream that ultimately led to her receipt of $91,000 from City of Springfield, Missouri, in 2009. It is included as companion material to the fictional Vision Quest story by Rev. John Buehrens. The Vision Quest is as powerfully effective today as it was before the European influence became dominant on this continent, but only if its purpose and practice are understood. The editors hope to inspire our readers to participate in their own Vision Quests by sharing these glimpses into why this series of anthologies by Native and non-Native Americans is titled *Gifts of the Great Spirit*.)

Part I

November 12, 2005, Springfield, Missouri

This experience should be of interest. I didn't think of the lucid dream vision as mystical until I realized a great deal was learned in it, especially about the Indians' usage of energy. I will copy part of my notes dated October 17, 2005, exactly as I wrote them.

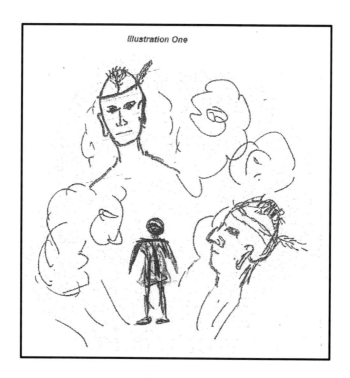

Illustration One

October 17, 2005

The sketches depict my silent dream/vision of five tall Native American males. Until I find my original notes, the date is unknown, but it must have been between May and early July 2005.

There was NO communication between us. I sensed they were showing me the site of a burial ground so. of Cherokee St. (in Springfield, Mo.) and in the 2000 block of So. Jefferson Ave., an area of single-family residences.

November 12, 2005

Before proceeding, I should add that the encounter took place before July 27, 2005, a date on which the city-hired contractor, Hartman Construction, turned off the water and began a major job that is still unfinished: tearing up the street to install new, bigger storm water drains, and to widen the road by taking parts of the front yards of a number of houses located in the same area it seemed the Indians were indicating was a burial-ground site.

If the construction crew dug up part or all of such a site, it was kept quiet; not a word appeared in the press.

At the last round of "repair," the city's own Public Works Dept. paved over the sanitary sewer manholes noted for spilling raw sewage into the street and yards--the ones I reported about. Such a burial will only be a temporary cure because sewage will back up into homes if it cannot get out any other way when a clog or flooding occurs.

So, the Indian men alerted me to "burial" and I photographed the site as a result, and now have Before-and-After photos to use in my legal matter known as *Parrott vs. City of Springfield*.

Further, local Ozarks historian Jim Barrett advised me in October that the Osage Indians, who lived here before white men forced their relocation, were tall, averaging six feet, and went almost nude in warm weather.

An old map I found in a paper file box in the Greene County archives, dated 1938, shows the location of an Osage settlement and burial grounds at a location I estimated to be about three blocks SE of my house and one mile due S, but if the encounter with the five male Indians was accurate, their site was actually within walking distance of my front yard.

HOW THEY FUNCTIONED
(Excerpts of Notes with sketches I drew after the encounter.)

General features--all men looked alike, but not exactly... Tall, lean, no fat... Skull shaped like an egg--sort of pointed at top and slanting back... Only a bit of hair on top (not enough to grab)... Spine--very straight... Skin--a tan, not dark, color... Nose--slight hump--sharp but not big...

They formed a cage by hunching upper torsos forward (I was in the center, perhaps like an animal on a hunt)... Locking arms around each other's' backs... Closing in so hip bones were almost touching... Then, rotating slowly in a circle (clockwise) as if rolling toward their destination--using what seemed to be many fast-but-small steps on the balls of their feet...

I didn't see (or recall) whether they wore foot coverings, but recall a head band and one feather. I think it was gray with white streaks... Lithe... Moved on balls of feet, (legs bent at knees, unlike the upright stance in my sketch – see next page).

Clad--brief leather--no frills... Outstanding in its detail was a leather thong wrapped around each Indian's wrist and from it dangled or hung a tool that could, with a flick of the wrist, fly up into the grip in such a way that the handle fit into the palm, around which the fingers grasped it for instant use. The handle was either wood or bone. Attached to it was a sharp blade. The tool, or weapon, looked like a small axe or modern-day meat cleaver. I believe the tool looked like a tomahawk. Whether it could be thrown like a tomahawk is not known. The leather bands to which each tool was attached were dark and about this width (IIIII), but the length to which it could be extended if the tools were thrown is unknown.

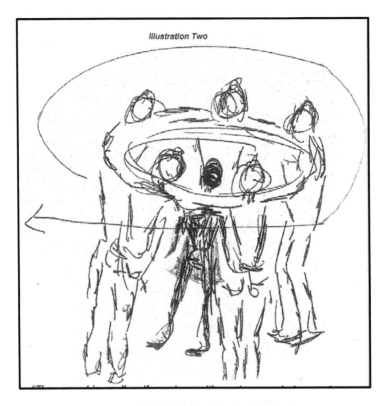

Illustration Two

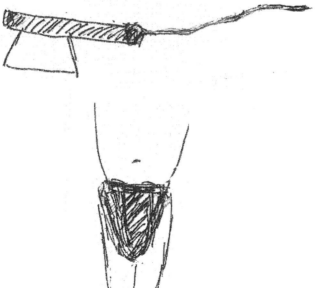

In my encounter, the men wore the bands tightly wrapped, and their bladed weapons were pressed against the heels of their hands (on the palm side at the wrist). In other words, they were not in use.

Other Facts

I was in the borderline state, as if dreaming.

They materialized as if out of *Prima Materia* like mist rising up and out of ground.

They surrounded me.

They entered silently into a well-orchestrated sort of dance in which they coordinated in one smooth, amazingly "light" and gracefully powerful movement that had the effect of teleporting me from one location to another.

As their circle sped up, they moved like one body, with me in the center. They did not touch or carry me, but the velocity of their rotating energy had the effect of making (it) as easy to move me as it would have been to transport a feather. I was trapped but had no fear, nor did I sense any hostility or other emotion from them.

Illustration Three

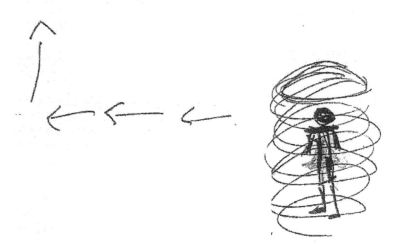

When the destination was reached, they dissipated back into shafts of mist-like energy and sank into the ground, leaving me with the impression that South Jefferson Avenue was a burial site.

Outcome

Ultimate outcome was that in September (2005) I addressed my city councilman (John D. Wylie) at a Neighborhood Public Meeting with the suggestion the area be declared a historic site and I am thinking of applying to the federal government for a Trail of Tears marker on my land.

Part II

IMPRESSIONS--VISIONS
(after the Experience)

1. The unadorned Indians wore only the feather as a symbol, like a badge, and, as such, were guardians of their sacred place. The nakedness was a symbol of Spirit in purest form.

2. I did not sense either intent or will from these Indians. It was as if, in my quest to know, I summoned them as a means of reading the *Book of Life.*

3. Knowledge I gained also included the way they used energy, which may be a simple key to the various Indian dances' purposes and practical applications.

Example: The Hunt

Using the same formation in which I underwent being transported, the "cage," a circle of hunters could have closed in on an animal. The number of hunters may have varied, but the ritual did not. They formed a circle around the prey. Then, with arms out but not touching each other, they moved in a dance of great precision, starting to crouch as they moved to make the circle grow smaller. They probably vocalized to accompany movement, but I heard no sounds in my vision.

By hunching over and crouching, while always moving, the prey was trapped and its senses were confused, so it paused to get its bearings, rather than striking, and in all likelihood, it crouched

As the Indians came together and closed the circle, they locked arms and the tops of their heads formed a dome or cover. Their circle began moving clockwise faster and faster as they bent lower and lower, where they were able to subdue or kill the bear, lion, or person, or bind it alive and carry it away bound in thongs.

Part III

THE OUTCOME

The turning point in the case I was building, both as neighborhood watch representative in "Springfieldians Against Storm Water/Sewage (SASS)" and as a private citizen whose property and health were virtually destroyed, came from the encounter with the five Osage spirits.

The spirit guides took me to a location I revisited during normal waking hours and gathered physical evidence to finish investigation into Springfield's failure to provide safe sanitation and water to its residents.

Because members of SASS dragged their feet about filing a Class Action against the City, I resigned to pursue settlement before I went broke, got too old, or died. I did public readings from my poetry chapbook about the contemporary tragedy along the historic route the Cherokees took en route to Oklahoma in 1839 and began garnering media attention. The spotlight began to turn on Springfield in what could have proven highly unfavorable publicity for the city touted as a great place to retire.

I don't claim to be Cherokee, but know I have a distant Chickasaw ancestor, so entitled my exposé, *THE LAST INDIAN ON THE TRAIL OF TEARS*. It contains the story of the five Osage hunters and other Native American spirit guides who helped me win my one-woman stand against City Hall without ever filing my case in court. By the time my former neighbors decided to take action in 2010, it was too late, and they went down the metaphorical drain.

In 2009, the city bought me out for $91,000 and I hit the trail for California. I used part of the proceeds to found the White Buffalo Native American Poet Laureate Contest, winners of which appear in this anthology.

In 2010, *THE LAST INDIAN ON THE TRAIL OF TEARS* won the IRWIN Award from Book Publicists of Southern California for best visionary campaign. Copies are available for $10 from WSP Literary Fund, P. O. Box 1821, Monterey, CA 93942-1821. Proceeds benefit White Buffalo projects co-produced by Barbara Callahan Quin (aka Little Crow Walking Eagle) through Great Spirit Publishing.

Never underestimate the power of Vision Quest!

(The final report to SASS, including evidence that resulted from the information gained from the Osage spirits, appears as a public service at FUNGUS AMUNGUS on Wanda Sue Parrott's website at www.amykitchenerfdn.org)

Also included in the report is FLOODVILLE, U.S.A., a haiku scroll with photographic illustrations of storm water flooding and raw sewage spills in the streets of Springfield, Missouri, by SASS members Wanda Sue Parrott and Albert L. Baker.

Wanda Sue Parrott shares techniques that helped her win in *Cutting Through Bureaucratic Red Tape--THE BOONDOGGLER'S BIBLE--How to Fight Like City Hall to Win!!* to be released in spring 2014 by Great Spirit Publishing). ❖

VISION QUEST III:

The Legend of the True Heart

Barbara Callahan Quin

White Feather, speaking to Little Crow Walking Eagle, told of the Legend of True Heart and the Knowing of Source (Great Spirit):

"True Heart supplied all the necessary nourishment to the Great Body," White Feather began. "It was perfectly located to do this job, right in the center of the Great Body.

"True Heart was strong – soft and firm at the same time. All its parts worked in harmony to send the Life Force all through the Great Body. Its muscles worked with perfect timing: up and down, back and forth, in and out, open and close, with a rhythm that was strong and gentle, singing like a lullaby and heard all through the Great Body.

"The Life Source flowed freely through the Great Body, unrestricted, to the Farthest Reaches and back again to the True Heart. Life was good and the Great Body grew. The Mind of the Great Body accepted the Gifts from the True Heart with gratitude and thanksgiving and was rewarded with an abundance of rich ideas and colorful thoughts. The Great Body was filled with Light and Love and sustained by the free-flowing Life Source.

"Time passed. One day, the True Heart became aware of its own existence. It realized what it was doing and the control that it had over the Great Body. It became aware of the Mind and the Farthest Reaches of the Great Body, and that they depended on the Life Source being sent to them for their existence. Only the True Heart could do this.

"True Heart became proud of its function and soon realized how hard it was working. There was never a moment's rest, for it was constantly pumping, surging, and singing the Life Source throughout the Great Body. It soon seemed that the Great Body was requiring more and more of the Life Source. True Heart became aware of the nature of the Life Source as it flowed in and out and from and throughout the True Heart. True Heart began to wonder and question where the Life Source came from. As it felt the demands of the Great Body growing, True Heart began to worry about being able to supply enough of the Life Source to the Farthest Reaches of the Great Body.

"'*What if I exhaust my supply of the Life Source?*' True Heart began to question. '*What will happen then? How will the Great Body survive? What will happen to Me? How shall I be sustained? Who will take care of Me?*'

"As the True Heart became more aware of its purpose, it became aware of constant motion within itself. True Heart wondered what if one of its channels collapsed and closed, no longer providing a way for the Life Source to flow? What if the Life Source stopped flowing? After all, True Heart didn't know where the Life Source came from."

"Where did it come from?" asked Little Crow Walking Eagle. White Feather smiled and continued.

"As True Heart's awareness and concerns grew, the Farthest Reaches of the Great Body began noticing a diminished supply of the Life Source. Activity slowed and Mind's ideas became less colorful and creative. Worry and concern took the place of Light and Love. True Heart began working against itSelf, struggling to push the Life Source through its channels, to pull it in from the outside. Its actions became slower. The ability of movement became constricted and the container housing the True Heart hardened. Several chambers stopped flowing and the Life Source was cut off from many areas of the Great Body altogether.

"The Great Body began to cry, because it knew that it was slowly dying and it did not understand the nature of death. Slowly, part by part, thought by thought, the Great Body ceased to thrive. Only here and there were there any signs of the Life Source, and they were hungry and guarded, fearful of being stolen away by the True Heart and given to another area of the Great Body. The Great Body lost awareness of itself as a whole and soon battled its parts over control of the Life Source that remained in diluted quantities. The True Heart worked harder now than ever before but could do nothing as it watched the Great Body shut down. One day, the True Heart lay down and worked no more."

"Then what happened?" Little Crow Walking Eagle asked, eyes wide.

"You are eager for answers," White Feather replied. "Do you not see that you are like the True Heart and that the Great Spirit that sustains you is the Life Source?

"As long as you allow the Life Source to flow freely through you, all parts of your Being will be blessed and prospered. Everyone will have enough--all they need. Your feet will dance and your hands will clap. Your Mind will sing with praises for the Life Source and your eyes will see the Beauty of the World as One.

"But if you suddenly begin to question whether the Life Source is flowing through you, that very doubt will restrict its flow in your life. True Heart became proud of its function, which is worthy as an awareness, but True Heart began to think it was doing all the work by itself, and that it had to be responsible for the flow of the Life Source that sustained it, that it had to control the function of the Great Body, because it didn't know if the Life Source would make it to the Farthest Reaches.

"When the True Heart stopped trusting the flow of the Life Source, it became fearful and that fear caused it to become unable to operate as it was created to do."

"The True Heart did not trust the Life Source?" asked Little Crow Walking Eagle.

"Yes," said White Feather.

"What happened next? Did the Great Body die?"

"The Farthest Reaches of the Great Body mourned the True Heart for a while and they continued to battle each other, blaming one another for the loss of the True Heart.

"But then one day they stopped fighting and began to remember what it was like before, when the Life Source was flowing freely to all parts of the Great Body, when all parts worked together for the good of the Whole. Even though it was difficult at first, they continued to remember. Instead of battling, they remembered."

White Feather paused and nodded, looking across the tree tops toward the blue of the sky.

"Then one day," said White Feather, nodding, index finger pointing upwards, "one day, the Remembering touched the True Heart and it was like awaking from a dream. Suddenly, the True Heart remembered, too! It became aware again of the Life Source that had seemed to be dormant for so long. The True Heart remembered all that the Life Source had done for it without ever making any demands other than the True Heart be an open channel for the Life Source to flow through freely.

"The True Heart began to grow stronger, as it became more thankful for the presence of the Life Source flowing through it and made Gratitude its way of life. True Heart let go of its pride and fear and its need to control the Flow, and just allowed the Life Source to Flow the best way that it knew how to do--fully and completely-- through the True Heart and to all the Farthest Reaches of the Great Body." ❖

A NOTE FROM THE EDITORS

Gifts of the Great Spirit, Volume IV, is full of interesting ideas, thought-provoking questions, heart-healing answers, and a lot more every time you re-read it. We encourage you to read with an open mind and acknowledge what the Great Spirit may be saying to you through these words.

Inspiration comes in many forms; we find offering the literary challenge invites the Creative Muse to awaken and ponder, what if...? What if it happened this way? What if I looked at it that way?

The Great Spirit knows no boundaries to the creation unfolding beneath its power. Great Spirit Publishing is proud to work with Amy Kitchener's Angels Without Wings Fdn./Wanda Sue Parrott, with assistance by Yvonne Londres, to bring you these unique poems and stories. We don't intend to prove any of them; we don't have to. The Great Spirit has spoken, and the reader will have to be the judge as to what he or she is willing to entertain in the realms of possibility.

One thing we know for sure: the Great Spirit speaks through everyone. All we have to do is be open and receptive to the messages intended for us. They can come from anywhere.

In fact, what is the Great Spirit saying to you.... right now? How will you respond? Will you take up the challenge to listen?

Blessings and Aho!*

(**Aho* is one form of Native American greeting and blessing, as intended here; it does also have other meanings in other languages.)

The White Buffalo Tribe

Len Fairchuk   Wanda Sue Parrott (aka Prairie Flower)

In the **White Buffalo Tribe**, Prairie Flower (Wanda Sue Parrott) is a successor to the late-great Canadian artist/ musician William Leonard Fairchuk, more familiarly known as Len "White Buffalo" Fairchuk. A Salteaux, Len named Wanda Sue as Honorary Chief of the White Buffalo in 1968 in Los Angeles (center picture above). Len celebrated talented Canadian First Nation people through his widely popular TV program "The Western Hour." Len died in 2004 and was posthumously inducted into the Aboriginal Music Hall of Fame.

The White Buffalo Tribe is true sponsor of the **Native American Poet Laureate poetry contest**. It is not a physical organization, although its lodge members and honorary chiefs are physical people. There are no officers, dues, meetings, bylaws, or rules. Only one way to join exists at present, as far as we know: each member finds at least one successor and initiates him/her in whatever manner is fitting. They serve in the *creative* spirit and *spiritual intention* of the Great Spirit, regardless of actual Native American descent.

Wanda Sue Parrott/Prairie Flower initiates her successors through literary nominations:

- Barbara Youngblood Carr, the first White Buffalo Poet Laureate award winner in 2009;
- Dr. Carl B. Reed, White Buffalo Poet Laureate award winner in 2010;
- Ronald J. Jorgenson, aka Dr. Charles A. Stone, White Buffalo Poet Laureate award winner in 2011;
- Neal "Badger Bob White" Whitman, White Buffalo Poet Laureate award winner in 2012;
- Gail Denham, White Buffalo Poet Laureate award winner in 2013.

As laureate poet, each became an Honorary Chief of the White Buffalo Tribe. Three others Wanda named were Barbara Callahan Quin (Little Crow Walking Eagle) and Yvonne Londres (Dances with Poetry), and William Childress.

Each initiate receives a symbolic Native American name by whatever means is appropriate, if he/she does not already have one. Prairie Flower's name came intuitively. She had a Chickasaw ancestor and possibly at least one Cherokee on her father's side, but there is no existing proof other than her late Aunt Geneve Stephenson's genealogy records that are incomplete. Her father was a cloud and shape reader and she has always been intuitive and attuned to various Native American numinous influences of a subtle nature.

The White Buffalo Native American Poet Laureate Program

Wanda Sue Parrott, working with Barbara Callahan Quin and Yvonne Londres, organized the first formal White Buffalo Native American Poet Laureate poetry competition in 2010. It is a growing challenge to pick the top winners each year as the quality of entries continues to improve and develop the voice intended to represent the Great Spirit.

The 2010 White Buffalo Native American Poet Laureate was **Dr. Carl B. Reed**, of Altus, Oklahoma, for his poem, "*The Poet and I.*" *Two* White Buffalo Calf Awards were given to Barbara Youngblood Carr, Austin, Texas, for her poem, "*Dreamdancing Back to Kituwha, Holy Birth Place of the Cherokee,*" and Dr. Charles A. Stone, Austin, Texas, for his poem, "*Maiden Rock.*"

The 2011 contest brought over 80 poet laureate entries, resulting in the 2011 White Buffalo Native American Poet Laureate award going to **Dr. Charles A. Stone**, of Austin, Texas, for his poem, "*Grandfather Cypress.*" Two 2011 White Buffalo Calf Awards were given to Ella Cather-Davis, New Richmond, Ohio, for her poem, "*The Four Winds' Song*"; and Hilda F. Wales, Albuquerque, New Mexico, for her poem, "*Familiar Path.*" The quality of entries inspired the judges to add two Third Place and four Fourth Place categories, plus nine additional online honorable mentions.

The 2012 White Buffalo Native American Poet Laureate was **Neal "Badger Bob White" Whitman**, of Pacific Grove, California, for his poem, "*Seven Ways to Prepare for Lengthening Days.*" Two 2012 White Buffalo Calf Awards were given to Dr. Charles A. Stone for his poem, "*One Feather, Two Skies,*" and Cindy Bechtold for her poem, "*Wisdom.*" There were five Peace Pipe Honorable Mention (Third Place), five Chief's Choice (Fourth Place) categories, plus nine Silver Sage awards (additional online honorable mentions).

The 2013 White Buffalo Native American Poet Laureate is **Gail Denham**, of Sunriver, Oregon, for her poem, *"We Run, the Deer and I."* Two 2013 White Buffalo Calf Awards were given to Carol Leavitt Altieri for her poem, *"Molly Ockett, Indian Doctress,"* and Lee Pelham Cotton for her poem, *"White Man's Foot, White Man's Flies."* There are two Peace Pipe Honorable Mention (Third Place), two Chief's Choice (Fourth Place) categories, plus five Silver Sage awards (additional online honorable mentions). The complete list of 2013 winners appears in the front of this book.

Judges for the 2010-2013 contests were Yvonne Londres, aka Dances with Poetry, and Barbara Callahan Quin, aka Little Crow Walking Eagle. The winning poems from 2010 plus the Unknown Namesake contributions were published as Volume I of *Gifts of the Great Spirit*. The winning poems from 2011 plus the Name the Chief contributions were published as Volume II of *Gifts of the Great Spirit*. The winning poems from 2012 plus the Dream Catcher of the White Buffalo contributions were published as Volume III of *Gifts of the Great Spirit*. The winning poems from 2013 plus the Legends contributions are published as Volume IV of *Gifts of the Great Spirit*.

All four volumes are sold online through Great Spirit Publishing, CreateSpace, Amazon, and Amazon Kindle, as well as via notice published in **The Dip*lo*emat**, official newsletter of Amy Kitchener's Angels Without Wings Foundation, whose founder and editor Wanda Sue Parrott (aka Prairie Flower) was co-sponsor of the 2010 contest, and who served as Contest Coordinator of the 2010-2013 contests.

SUMMARY OF CONTENTS

Page #   Title - Author's Name

ALSO AVAILABLE FROM

GREAT SPIRIT PUBLISHING

Great Spirit Publishing is proud to bring you entertaining and mind-expanding literary works from known and unknown writers. These additional products may be of interest to you; Contact Great Spirit Publishing directly for ordering information by sending an e-mail to us at greatspiritpublishing@yahoo.com, or visit us online at www.greatspiritpublishing.yolasite.com/book-store.php, www.amazon.com, or www.createspace.com.

Dear Jude –
Jeanne Marie Olin
Jessie moves from the Midwest to San Francisco in the 1960s, where life is hip and cool - - and dangerous! Can St. Jude and Detective Joe Anthony catch a criminal intent on making Jessie his next victim?
ISBN – 13: 978-1490931654;$14 – Order: www.createspace.com/4352225

MIND According to Logos – *the Brain Reveals Its Own Secrets* – *A. Irving Rosenberg, Esq.*
Is it possible the endocrine glands of the human body are the portal to spiritual awakening? This book is based on thirty years of research and correspondence by Wanda Sue Parrott and retired attorney A. Irving Rosenberg.
ISBN – 13:978-1482375053; $14 – Order: www.createspace.com/4161813

Golden Words: Fine Poetry by American Poets 50 and Older – *edited by Wanda Sue Parrott -* 19th edition (20th Anniversary) features 2012 Senior Poets Laureate poetry competition winners first-round finalists list. Sponsor: Amy Kitchener's Angels without Wings Fdn., Monterey, Ca.
ISBN – 13: 978-1480014121: $18 – Order: www.createspace.com/4011830.

Iron Lotus: Memoirs of Sumi Sevilla Haru
– Sumi Sevilla Haru
Inspiring story of Asian American woman who is an actress, television and festival producer, journalist, community leader, and the first and only Asian American to serve as Vice-President of the AFL-CIO.
ISBN – 13: 978-1479331536: $18 – Order: www.createspace.com/3998707.

Too Close to the Su
— Laureen Kruse Diephof
Journey with Dutch boy
Wim Diephof on his
journey to manhood
during World War II in
the course of his
participation in the Dutch resistance.
ISBN–13: 978-1475002041: $18;
Order www.createspace.com/3819589.

How to Build a Penny Pyramid - *Volume I in the Shortcuts to Success Series: Seed Coins in a Nutshell - Wanda Sue Parrott*
Based on John D.
Rockefeller's money secrets,
symbology of the Great Pyramid, and
Pythagorean geometry, this creative
money management system is safe,
easy, and legal.
ISBN – 13: 978-1467917599: $15 –
Order: www.createspace.com/3720652.

How to Enter – and WIN – Poetry Contests – *Shortcuts to Success Series edition with Secrets of the Seven Lucky Letters ~ Wanda Sue Parrott*
Tips and techniques to aid you to
becoming an award-winning contestant
in poetry contests. Grammar, forms,
examples, and more from award-
winning poet, writer, and journalist
Wanda Sue Parrott.
ISBN – 13: 978-1466478619: $13 –
Order: www.createspace.com/3714241.

Gifts of the Great Spirit *(Volume IV) - Legends - edited by Wanda Sue Parrott and Barbara Quin*
ISBN-13: 978-1490916200: $15 –
Order:
www.createspace.com/4349899.

Gifts of the Great Spirit *(Volume III) - Dream Catcher of the White Buffalo - edited by Wanda Sue Parrott and Barbara Quin*
ISBN-13: 978-1477588154: $15 –
Order: www.createspace.com/3897299.

Gifts of the Great Spirit *(Volume II) – to the Spirit of the White Buffalo – edited by Wanda Sue Parrott and Barbara Quin*
ISBN- 13: 978-1466351936: $15 –
Order: www.createspace.com/3692263.

Gifts of the Great Spirit *(Volume I) - from White Buffalo to the Unknown Namesake - edited by Wanda Sue Parrott and Barbara Quin*
ISBN-13: 978-1452820842: $13 – Order:
www.createspace.com/3448329.

Find More Online at: www.greatspiritpublishing.yolasite.com
All titles also available on www.amazon.com.

CONTACT GREAT SPIRIT PUBLISHING IF:

- You want to order any of these items directly from Great Spirit Publishing (payment option available through PayPal or via "snail mail");

- You want to know what is available for free in the form of e-books and inspiring graphics to print and display; or

- You would like to be put on a mailing list to receive notice of future similar publications by these authors and/or this publisher.

Send an e-mail request to greatspiritpublishing@yahoo.com.

independent publishing technologies

www.greatspiritpublishing.yolasite.com

greatspiritpublishing@yahoo.com

Made in the USA
Middletown, DE
09 January 2023

20894356R00075